The Kings of
BLACK MAGIC

The Kings of
BLACK MAGIC

by I. G. EDMONDS

❖❖❖❖❖

illustrated with photographs

Holt, Rinehart and Winston ❖ New York

Picture Sources

Pages 11 and 46: The photos of the Sphinx and of the ruins of Ephesus were taken by the author.

Pages 38, 110, and 114: The Indian fakir woodcut and the portraits of Cagliostro and Seraphina Cagliostro are from the Houdini Collection in the Library of Congress.

Pages 51, 63, 74, and 79: The woodcuts of Julian the Apostate, Agrippa, Paracelsus, and Trithemius are from the Library of Congress.

Page 82: The etching of Faust by Rembrandt is from the Los Angeles Public Library.

Page 99: The portrait of John Dee is from an original in the Ashmolean Museum, Oxford, England.

Pages 129 and 144: The portrait of Edward Bulwer-Lytton and the illustration from *Zanoni* are from Bulwer-Lytton's *Zanoni* (1882).

Page 156: The portrait of Eliphas Lévi is from *The French Sorcerer* (1903—the author is unknown).

Library of Congress Cataloging in Publication Data
Edmonds, I. G.   The kings of black magic.
Bibliography: p. 191. Includes index.
Summary: Brief biographies of some famous
practitioners of black magic throughout history.
Includes Johann Faust, Cagliostro, John Dee,
Edward Bulwer-Lytton, Aleister Crowley, and others.
1. Magicians—Biography—Juvenile literature.
[1. Magicians. 2. Witchcraft—Biography] I. Title.
BF1597.E35   133.4′092′2 [B] [920]   79-19534
ISBN 0-03-051376-6

For my daughter Annette

Contents

The Kings of
BLACK MAGIC

❖1❖

The World Beyond

In the dim years when beasts were becoming human, a hairy, stooped brute with a club in his hand stalked his prey along the game trails of a savage world.

Suddenly a rock slipped in the cliff above him. It fell with a crash that frightened the prey and narrowly missed crushing the hunter. The caveman looked up fearfully, but there was no one on the cliff who could have dislodged the stone. It was as if the rock had a life of its own and had moved of its own accord.

In a similar manner, this creature, the forefather of man, saw gentle breezes change into raging storms that swept violently across his world. Sometimes fire burst from the mountains and stones were hurled into the sky by the volcanic fury. Small streams became rushing torrents. At other times the earth shook, heaved, and split. The torn sides sometimes rose so high in the air that new mountains were created.

The caveman was different from the beasts of his time. His brain was larger in relation to his size. He had imagination, a sense of wonder, and a hunger to know why things happened. His gradually expanding mind demanded a reason for the strange things that went on in his world.

His fumbling reason began to realize that some aspects of the natural world tried to help him and other aspects tried to do him harm. This tremendous realization was the seed from which magic grew. Magic is the art of controlling natural or supernatural forces by charms, spells, and rituals. Magic in turn led to religion, science, and culture. None of these things would have come about if the human brain had not been puzzled by unexplained things that it observed.

These first questions about the nature of things led to *animism*. This is the belief that natural objects, like rocks, trees, the wind, and such, have spirits or souls. Early mankind reasoned that this must be so. If this were not true, then how could rocks move, the wind blow, clouds sweep across the sky, and volcanoes erupt?

The next step was to divide these spirits into good and bad, according to whether they aided or tried to destroy him.

Animism was the first attempt to explain the unknown and the beginning of *occultism,* the study of the world beyond.

Once the developing mind of early people realized that there was an unknown world beyond the normal senses, the next logical step was for more intelligent members of the tribe to attempt to interpret and explain the occult. Then from simple explaining, these first priests and priestesses, soothsayers and witch doctors became mediators between humanity and the spirits who dwelled in the earth and its objects.

The primitive mind could not visualize the unknown. The early humans knew the unknown was there, but the priests and priestesses of the animistic period could describe the unknown only in terms of what they knew. This is still true today, but we know more today and have a wider range with which to make comparisons.

Comparison is the only way we can describe anything. We say something has a trunk *like* an elephant. Or that it shakes *like* jelly. If the object we wish to describe resembles nothing we have ever seen, it is impossible to describe it. The primitive mind was in exactly this position when it attempted to explain the unknown world of the occult to the rest of the tribe. Thus primitive man's concept of gods, spirits, ghosts, devils, and other supernatural phenomena was based upon what he knew in terms of his fellow man, animals, and natural objects.

Since these spirits were on a plane removed from man, they naturally were conceived as being larger, mightier, and more all-knowing than ordinary people and things.

Thus the great god became in the minds of primitive people a more powerful model of the tribal leader raised to a supernatural plane. The devils became a compilation of all the human and animal wickedness the people were familiar with.

The realization that there is good and evil on a spiritual plane caused a split in ancient magic. This created what became known as black magic and white magic. White magic led to formal religion. At first the various religions were pagan, but gradually expanded into more sublime concepts. Black magic continued to lean to the supernatural and the occult. It was classed as "evil" by those who followed formal religions.

While formal religions have taken many different roads, black magic has remained closer to its origin. Those who practice it today use much the same rituals, rites, and incantations that have been handed down from prehistoric witch doctors through men like John Dee, Johann Faust, Edward Kelley, Cagliostro, and Aleister Crowley.

Black magic, in its true form, is not Satanism, necromancy, or sorcery, although practitioners of these darker arts may use magic as a key to the sinister side of the occult. *Satanism* is devil worship. *Necromancy* is the use of the dead for prophecy, although the word has become a synonym for sorcery in the public mind. *Sorcery* is the use of evil powers to influence and control people and events.

The true student of black magic, in contrast to Satanists and sorcerers, is a scientist of the occult. Such students are not devil worshipers. Nor do they brew witches' love potions or murder their enemies by sticking pins in effigies. These students seek occult knowledge and the truth behind the unknown. Like all true scientists, they are trying to push back the frontier of human knowledge, but on a different plane from that of ordinary scientists.

Failing to find the occult knowledge they sought through legitimate means, many students of magic turned to more sinister forces. The classic example, of course, is Faust, the man who sold his soul to the devil.

John Dee, the magician who served Queen Elizabeth I, was among the most learned men of his time. When he found his search for the occult blocked, he also turned to the supernatural. Unlike Faust, Dee turned to Heaven and asked the angels to teach him the secrets of the unknown.

Dee summed up the feelings of all true students of the occult when he wrote:

> All my lifetime I had spent in learning. I have done this for forty years continually, in many manners and in many countries. I found at length that neither any man living, nor any book I could yet find, was able to teach me the truths I sought and longed for.
>
> Therefore I concluded with myself to make intercession and prayer to the Giver of Wisdom and All Good Things, to send me such wisdom, as I might know the natures of His creatures; and also enjoy means to use them to His honor and glory.

Practically all the great students of magic have found themselves in this same situation. Although Dee preferred to turn to Heaven, he ended up in association with one of the greatest rascals in the history of black magic, the infamous Edward Kelley.

Other students of black magic were like the notorious Cagliostro. He was a rascal and thief who studied magic under the peculiar Comte de Saint-Germain in order to expand his knavery. An even worse person was Aleister Crowley, who delighted in being called "the wickedest man in the world." Crowley was an ardent and sincere student of black magic until he found that he could not penetrate the veil of the unknown. Then, rather than admit defeat to his followers, he resorted to outrageous trickery.

The true students of magic—men like John Dee in his younger days and Edward Bulwer-Lytton (author of *The Last Days of Pompeii)* all of his life—in their role of occult scientist were concerned with demons and spirits only to prove whether there were or were not such things. The difference between these people and men like Cagliostro and Crowley is the difference between Einstein pushing back the frontiers of physics with $E = MC^2$ and the technicians at the Manhattan Project, who used Einstein's formula to build the first atomic bomb.

While magic itself goes back to the fumbling attempts of primitive people to explain natural wonders, the word magic comes from ancient Persia. It is said that the Persians got the word *maghdim,* which means wisdom, from the Chaldeans. The fire-worshiping priests of Persia became known as *magi,* and from this source comes the word magician. The three wise men who brought gifts to the Christ child were magi.

The Persians were invaders. They were part of the great migration of the Aryan people from the steppes of Asia. These people divided and settled in widely separated places in Europe and Asia. Nothing is known of them except that they had light skins and spoke a language known today as Indo-European. This language is the root of all European languages except Albanian, Basque, Estonian, Finnish, Hungarian, and Turkic. Hindi, the language of India, also came from an Aryan root.

The Aryans took their name from *aryas,* a Sanskrit word that means nobles. Little is known about the other branches, but the Aryans who invaded India about 1500 B.C. were responsible for the world's oldest books of a living religion. These books are *The Vedas,* which were the foundation of today's Hinduism. *Veda* means knowledge.

Sometime around the year A.D. 40 the Greek magician Apollonius of Tyana went to India. There the Hindu sage Iarchas told the Greek visitor that the Egyptians learned their magic from the Hindus.

The early Vedic religion was close to primitive animism. Its followers worshiped nature gods, and their worship was filled with magical rituals. The hymns of the Vedas, written to ensure the magical blessings of these gods, are among the most beautiful ever written.

The hymn to ensure the continued heat of the sun begins:

Behold the rays of Dawn, like heralds,
   lead on high,
The Sun, that men may see the great
   all-knowing god.
The Stars slink off like thieves, in company
   with Night,
Before the all-seeing eye, whose beams reveal
   his presence.

The hymn to Indra, god of both storm and war, was sung to ensure rain:

Vainly the demon dares thy might, in vain
Strives to deprive us of thy watery treasure.
Earth quakes beneath the crashing of thy bolts.
Pierced, shattered lies the foe—his cities crushed.
His armies overthrown, his fortresses
Shivered to fragments; then the pent-up waters,
Released from long imprisonment, descend
In torrents to the earth, and swollen rivers
Foaming and rolling to their ocean-home,
Proclaim the triumph of you, O Thunderer.
(translation by Morier Morier-Williams, 1877)

Evidently these early Aryans made human sacrifices to their gods. This destroyed too many youths needed to fight the Aryans' enemies. So, either through the magic of the Vedic priests or the compassion of the god Indra, human souls passed into horses. This permitted the sacrifice of horses in the place of young men and women.

The horse sacrifice was extremely important; it magically assured the protection of the gods for another year. A white horse was selected, for white is the symbol of purity. The horse had to be without blemish. He was turned loose to wander where he wished for a year. Soldiers followed to see that no person hindered or harmed the sacred animal. At the end of the year, the horse was brought back. Its throat was cut and the blood caught to use in magic rites.

If we can believe Iarchas' claim that his people taught magic and philosophy to the Egyptians and Chaldeans, then the Aryans were the first civilized people to use magic, the true forefathers of Johann Faust, John Dee, Apollonius of Tyana, Eliphas Lévi, Cagliostro, MacGregor Mathers, Aleister Crowley, and all the other great magicians who have sought to unveil the unknown through the incantations, rituals, and pentagrams of magic. Pentagrams are magical diagrams drawn by magicians to aid and control their magic.

Despite Iarchas' claim that the Hindus originated magic, the oldest book of magic is the fabled *Book of Thoth*, named for the Egyptian god of magic. This book is so old that it was already a legend in the time of Cheops, who built the Great Pyramid of Giza about 2500 B.C., a thousand years before the Aryans came to India.

A crumbling papyrus manuscript tells how Cheops

once sought information from the *Book of Thoth*. He was told that Thoth, angry because some mortals had earlier stolen the book, had it placed in a series of nested boxes and cast into the Red Sea.

The Great Pyramid itself is believed by many to be a magical object. A large following has grown up for what has been termed pyramidology. These followers see magic in every stone, and claim that proper measurement of the great gallery gives the history and future of mankind.

Far more mysterious than the pyramids is the Sphinx of Giza. This lion-bodied, woman-headed colossus was carved from local rock by unknown persons long before the pyramids were built. The Sphinx is 75 feet high and 150 feet long; the head alone is 30 feet long and the face is 14 feet wide. Although the layers of granite rock from which it is carved give the appearance of built-up rock, the Sphinx is solid. Its base extends up the native rock.

The Sphinx is so old that there is not even a good legend to tell us how it was carved, who did it, or why. We do know that it must have been ancient when Cheops built the Great Pyramid, for there is a record that he had the Sphinx repaired.

We also know that the Sphinx was almost covered with sand between 1600 B.C. and 1400 B.C. Only its head protruded above the sand. A young prince had a strange adventure at the site. He had the story carved on a slab of stone and placed between the paws of the Sphinx. It is still there for us to read today.

A plaque between the paws of the Sphinx tells how Thothmes IV became pharaoh of Egypt.

According to the story, the prince was out hunting. He grew tired and stopped to rest in the shadow of the Sphinx's head. He fell asleep and dreamed that the stone head spoke to him. The Sphinx promised that if the prince had the sand dug away from her body, she would make him pharaoh of Egypt. He did. Although he was not next in the line of succession, all in front of him died, and he became pharaoh under the reigning name of Thothmes IV.

Magic was a vital part of Egyptian religion. It guided a person from birth rites to the final journey of the soul to be judged. This total reliance on magic made the priests very powerful. The priests of the Nile were also the ones who introduced trickery in magic rites. This trickery later led to the branch of magic that developed into stage magic or conjuring. Many of the tricks used by today's stage magicians originated in ancient Egypt.

But in old Egypt magic trickery was done not for amusement but to awe the temple worshipers. True magic is not always impressive, nor does it work on schedule. The priests needed something they could control—something awesome that would prove they did communicate with the gods.

Although they resorted to tricks to awe the populace, these ancient priests probably really believed in their gods. Being educated, they could support their beliefs, as we do today, on faith. The uneducated populace needed some visible signs, and this necessitated trickery.

Many of these temple tricks used true science. The priests boiled water and used steam pressure to open huge doors mysteriously. Burnished mirrors reflected the images of priests' faces on smoke screens to make "god's" face on the writhing smoke. Unusual lighting effects caused priests to appear out of nowhere and then to vanish in a mysterious manner.

An old papyrus tells of a magician who could cut off a bird's head and restore it. The secret of this trick has survived the ages. Stage magicians have used it ever since.

Some fowl sleep with their heads tucked under their wings. All that is necessary to do the head-cutting trick is to teach the bird to hold this pose. Then the magician uses a carved and painted head just like the bird's head. Feathers are glued on and the neck painted red to simulate the bloody cut. This fake head is palmed by the magician as he goes through the motions of cutting off the bird's head. Under cover of his actions, he tucks the live bird's head down under its wing (the one turned away from the audience) and holds up the dummy cut head for all to see. Now to restore the bird's head, he momentarily blocks the audience's view with his hand, palming the fake head and lifting up the real head from its place under the wing.

In introducing trickery into ritual magic, the Egyptian priests set a precedent for a horde of magicians who followed them. In fact, there has been so much trickery and fraud in the name of magic that it is extremely difficult to separate the sincere magician, whom we call "an occult scientist," from the legion of fakers who have deluded the public and sometimes themselves for at least five thousand years—and heaven only knows how many years before that.

Even so, there have been many sincere students of magic. Sincerity, of course, is not always proof of truth, but it is proof that the magician is genuinely trying to find the truth. A search for the sincere magicians is complicated by the fact that some of the most sincere students of magic turned to fakery when they found that they lacked the power to be true magicians. Cagliostro was one of these. Crowley—the Beast 666—was another. But this does not lessen the fact that at one time they were sincere students. On the other end, someone like Bulwer-Lytton never tried to trick anyone. He spent a lifetime studying magic, but never openly revealed what he learned. He did hide it in a book he wrote "for those who can comprehend it."

The following accounts are of some of the people who at one time or another sincerely believed in black magic and tried earnestly to reveal its secrets.

❖2❖

The Fabulous Magicians

The earliest magicians who have come down to us by name were fabulous people—people whose lives are so clouded by fable that little is really known about them.

The first of these is Teta, whose story is told in the Westcar Papyrus, now in an East Berlin museum. Teta lived five thousand years ago in the days of Cheops, who built the Great Pyramid. In building his tomb, Cheops wanted to put above the lintel the *aptets* that Thoth, god of magic, placed on the walls of his own burial chamber.

Today no one knows what an *aptet* is. It may have been a symbol, an amulet, or a charm. However, they knew what it was in Cheops' day, but they did not know how many *aptets* Thoth had in his tomb. The secret was so old it had been lost centuries before Cheops was born.

Then the pharaoh heard of Teta, who had a great

reputation as a magician. Teta was then 110 years old and so feeble that he had to be carried from his home to the palace. He did know the number of *aptets* on the walls of the lost sanctuary of Thoth, and revealed the secret to the king. He also knew how to cut off the heads of birds and restore them to life. He used a goose to demonstrate this to the king and later did the same trick with an ox.

Another fabulous magician was Zaclas, who was a good detective. A man was killed, and his property taken by his young widow and her lover. The dead man's father was suspicious and sought help from Zaclas. There were no witnesses or evidence against the wife. So Zaclas used his magic. He burned incense, performed some strange movements with his hands, and spoke esoteric words that no one could understand. Then the spectators were struck with fearful astonishment as the dead man began to speak. He accused his wife of murdering him and fell back dead again.

Magicians then as now were not eager to reveal their secrets. We do not find much written about how they accomplished their arts. A lot of what we know about Egyptian magic comes from Greek writers. When the Greek classical age was just getting started, the Greeks looked to Egypt as a model. A pilgrimage to the land of the Nile was considered a finishing school for those studying philosophy.

A man was considered very fortunate if he could get the Egyptian priests to accept him as a student. One applicant spent ten years before he was accepted. It took this long for him to convince the priests of his sincerity.

The three greatest Greeks who studied in Egypt were Thales, Pythagoras, and Plato. Solon the Athenian also visited Egypt, but there is no record that he studied magic. The legend of lost Atlantis, the sunken continent, is based upon stories Solon supposedly heard from Egyptian priests.

According to this story, the Atlanteans, who lived on an island outside the Pillars of Hercules (Gibraltar), made war on the people of the Mediterranean Sea area. They conquered land as far eastward as Italy before being defeated in battle by the Athenians. Later this island kingdom was shaken by tremendous earthquakes and sank into the sea. Both Atlantis and the Atlantic Ocean get their names from the Greek god Atlas, who holds the world on his shoulders.

Thales, who lived about 640–546 B.C., was one of the Seven Wise Men of Greece. Historians have never agreed on who all these sixth century B.C. philosophers were, but Thales is on every list. He gained great fame by predicting the eclipse of the sun on May 28, 585 B.C. He is also credited with establishing the science of abstract geometry. His Egyptian studies were said to have influenced his work in astronomy and led to new theories on the nature of the basic principles of the universe.

Pythagoras, who lived from around 582–500 B.C., is generally regarded as having been initiated into the mysteries of Egyptian magic. These secrets, acquired over a period of twenty years' study, became part of the teaching of the Pythagorean school he founded in the Greek colony of Crotona, in southern Italy.

A lot has been written about Pythagoras and his beliefs. Yet nothing is really known about his true philosophy and magical art, for he wrote nothing himself. All we know of him comes from others. Since these writers are sometimes in conflict, it is generally believed that some of them put forth their own ideas. They cloaked them in Pythagoras' reputation to get their ideas more readily accepted.

The Pythagorean school was a mystical brotherhood that dealt with science, magic, and philosophy. Unfortunately, Pythagoras branched out into politics, resulting in his death and the burning of his school.

As near as we can determine, Pythagoras believed in reincarnation. He also believed in *numerology*, the occult science of numbers. His or his followers' work with numbers laid the foundation for all development in geometry that followed his time. High school students should remember the Pythagorean theorem: The square of the hypotenuse of a right-angled triangle is equal to the sum of the squares of the other two sides.

The Pythagoreans believed that all creation, including the sun, planets, and stars, revolved around a central fire. This movement was controlled by a system of numbers.

The most influential of the Greek philosophers was Plato (427–347 B.C.). For years he was a student of Socrates and recorded much of what we know of his master.

Paul Christian (in his *History and Practice of Magic,* 1870) tells something of Pythagoras' and Plato's magic studies in Egypt:

> Pythagoras had as his master the arch-prophet Sonchis. Plato, according to Proclus, was taught for thirteen years by the Magi Patheneitb, Ochoaps, Sechtnouphis, and Etymon of Sebennithis. And so the famous doctrine which has kept the word *platonic* and which has had such a great influence on the philosophical development of Christian ideas came originally from the sanctuaries of Memphis, the town of Menes, and from Heliopolis, the town of the sun. ["Christian" refers to Neoplatonism—the New Platonism—which developed in Alexandria in the beginning of the Christian era and deeply influenced early Christian writers.]

Neither Pythagoras nor Plato left any record of what he actually experienced in the dark temples of the Egyptian magicians. For this we must turn to Iamblicus, a Greek of the fourth century A.D., who wrote *De mysteriis aegyptorum,* a title usually translated as *On the Mysteries.* Actually, the original manuscript was unsigned. Proclus (412–485 A.D.) is the writer who identified Iamblicus as the author.

Iamblicus begins with a falsity. He claims that there was a bronze door between the paws of the Sphinx which could be opened only by a priest who knew the secret. The door led into a maze that wound to secret rooms under the Great Pyramid. The maze was so constructed that if any person who was not a member of the brotherhood got through the door, the maze would always lead him back to the door. He could never penetrate to the secret temple.

Careful searches have been made for secret doors, tunnels, and chambers in and around both the Sphinx and the Great Pyramid. Only recently there was an attempt to use radar to probe for secret chambers in the pyramid. None of these have found anything.

However, the Sphinx did not sit alone. There was a temple in front of it. The massive rocks and partial walls can still be seen today. So it is still possible that the strange rites recorded by Iamblicus took place in this temple, in some secret chamber. It has also been suggested that the applicants were led through a maze and told that they were taken under the pyramid as a precaution to hide the real location.

The book describes the initiation rites into the brotherhood, and it makes a weird tale indeed. These rites were supposed to be hermetic—that is, based upon the teachings of Thoth-Hermes, also known as Hermes Trismegistus (the Thrice Greatest). Thoth was originally the scribe of the Egyptian gods and later god of numbers and magic. Hermes was his Greek counterpart. The Greeks combined the two.

This was done in Alexandria, Egypt, the city Alexander the Great founded after he conquered Egypt in 332 B.C. Alexandria became the center of Greek culture in the Near East.

The Alexandrian Greeks attributed forty-two books of Egyptian magic to Thoth. These formed the basis of "hermetic magic." The ancient Egyptians, on the other hand, attributed only *The Book of Thoth* to the god of magic. In his book *Egyptian Magic* (1899), the Egyptologist E.A. Wallis Budge quotes a papyrus from the Ptolemaic period (323 B.C. to 30 B.C.) that talks about *The Book of Thoth.*

It tells of a man named Setnau who was skilled in magic. Once while discussing magic, Setnau was challenged by a courtier. The magician invited the skeptic to join him in hunting for the *Book of Thoth.* "In the book are two charms," Setnau said. "The first will enchant heaven, earth, hell, sea, and mountains. The second will enable a man if he be in the tomb to take the form that he had on earth."

The skeptic refused Setnau's challenge, but the magician set out with his brother to find the book. The book was supposed to be in the tomb of Ptah-nefer-ka in Memphis, the ancient Egyptian capital. The brothers searched for three days before they found the tomb. Budge writes:

> Setnau recited some words over it. The earth opened and they went into the ground. While Setnau had been told the book was in the tomb, he had never been here before. The two brothers

went on fearfully. After going through a dark passage, they emerged into a tomb room. The room was brilliantly lighted by an unearthly brilliance that came from a book.

In the tomb were the revived bodies of Ptah-nefer-ka and his wife and son. Setnau told them that he had come for the Book of Thoth. They could not prevent his taking it, but Ahura, the wife, warned Setnau that the book would bring him misfortune.

Ahura then told the story of how her husband got the book. A wicked priest agreed to tell Ptah-nefer-ka where the book was hidden in return for some silver and two coffins. The price was paid and the priest said that the book was hidden in an iron box sunk in the Nile River. The priest said:

> The iron box is in a bronze box, the bronze box is in a box of palm-tree wood, the palm-tree box is in a box of ebony and ivory, the ebony and ivory box is in a box of silver, the silver box is in a gold box. The box wherein is the book is surrounded by swarms of serpents and scorpions and reptiles of all kind, and around it is coiled a serpent that cannot die.

After asking the pharaoh's permission, Ptah-nefer-ka went in search of the nested boxes. He found them after three days of search, and used his own magic to destroy all the snakes and scorpions, except the one serpent which could not die. This snake kept coming back to life and attacking Ptah-nefer-ka as fast and as often as he killed it. Then through magic inspiration he found a way to confound this serpent. He hastily cut it in two pieces and piled sand between them so that the halves could not find each other and rejoin.

Ptah-nefer-ka read the magic formulae. The first revealed to him all the secrets of the heavens, earth, and hell. The second revealed to him how to restore his life after death. Then he copied the book onto a new papyrus, dissolved the paper in liquid, and drank it. This gave him all the knowledge in the *Book of Thoth.*

Now Thoth observed all this with anger. He complained to Ra, the sun god, who gave permission for Ptah-nefer-ka's death. The rash man, his wife and son all perished, but through the second secret he learned in the stolen *Book of Thoth,* he was able to bring back the doubles of himself, his wife and son. They lived again, but were prisoners in their tomb.

Setnau listened to Ahura's story but refused to heed the warning. He took the book and left, but so many troubles beset him that he returned the book on order of the pharaoh. This was in accordance with a prediction Ptah-nefer-ka made to Ahura when Setnau left with the magic book. Today Memphis is a ruins not far from the place where the fabulous Imhotep built the first step pyramid in Egypt, the forerunner of the pyramids at Giza. If there is any truth in the legends, somewhere under the sand is the tomb of Ptah-nefer-ka. He, his wife and son still live in it, their tomb world lighted by the brilliance from the *Book of Thoth.*

An initiation into the secret Hermetic Egyptian brotherhood was a soul-shaking experience, according to Iamblicus. The applicant was introduced to two guardians of the rites. The beginner was told that he must follow instructions to the letter if he valued his life. He was also told that any sign of weakness would result in his disqualification. In this case, he would be barred forever from taking the tests again.

The applicant's eyes were covered with a bandage. Then he was led through a succession of doors. He was suddenly stopped and told: "We are on the edge of a great precipice. The slightest step forward will plunge you to your death in the abyss. We must wait here for our brothers to lower a drawbridge. Do not move, if you value your life."

The blindfolded postulant waited in terror. Suddenly the blindfold was jerked from his eyes. The room was dark. Then a light came on in the back. It revealed a hideous ghost who swung a scythe at the trembling man, crying, "Woe to him who disturbs the dead!"

The ghost disappeared and the postulant was congratulated on his courage. Then he was asked if he wished to demonstrate that he could conquer vanity. When he answered yes, he was given a flickering torch and told to crawl through a narrow passageway.

It was so narrow he could barely squeeze through. This, he was told, was the symbol of the tomb. He crawled along, clutching the clay lamp with its flickering flame. At last the tunnel widened, but he discovered that it ended in a deep pit. There was an iron ladder descending into the hole. Bronze doors closed, preventing him from retreating into the tunnel. Clutching his lamp, he climbed to the bottom of the ladder. It ended at the twenty-third rung, with empty space below. Bewildered, trembling, sure that he had failed and that death awaited him, the postulant clung to the ladder.

Men who took these tests were not ordinary people. Applicants for initiation into the Egyptian mysteries had to be above the ordinary in intelligence or they could not have progressed through the initial training to this final initiation. After the first panic, they began to reason. There had to be a way out. Each was warned before beginning that this was a soul-shaking test of courage and faith. Each was told at the start: "Go without fear. You have only yourself to fear in this test of solitude."

Iamblicus tells us that at this point the postulant took heart. He held the lamp to try and see into the darkness below. There was no platform he could jump to. So he began moving slowly back up the iron ladder. The bronze doors were closed above, but he sought some opening that he might have missed in the pit walls. Or it was possible that some message of direction was carved there, providing instruction on what to do next. Inch by inch he feverishly searched for something to aid him in his distress. At the same time he had to worry about the oil running out in his clay lamp. This was a very pressing danger. If his light failed, he knew he could never find his way to safety in the total darkness of the closed pit. It now seemed, in spite of all efforts, that he was lost. Then as he moved slowly back up the ladder, he discovered an opening in the wall. He had missed it on his way down. He swung off the ladder into the opening. There were stairs inside. He climbed them and found his way blocked by a bronze grating.

Through the grating he could see a long gallery. It was lighted by eleven bronze tripods of burning oil. He could see a line of twenty-four small stone sphinxes. On the wall behind them were twenty-two paintings of a strange nature.

A magus who identified himself as "the guardian of the sacred symbols" appeared and opened the grating. The shivering postulant entered. The magus said, "Welcome, Son of Earth! You have discovered the path of wisdom and escaped the pit. Few have succeeded in doing this. Many before you have died in the attempt. Come and I will explain the arcana [secrets] of the sacred symbols."

The magus took the postulant and paused before each of the strange paintings. The first was of a magus depicted as a perfect man. He wore a long white robe girdled by a serpent belt. The buckle of the belt was the snake's head grasping its own tail. The magus in the picture held a scepter, and in front of him were a goblet, a sword, and a gold coin.

The magus explained the symbolism of the objects in the pictures. They passed on, the pictures becoming more strange as they proceeded. Some of the others showed such things as a door of occult sanctuary, the goddess Isis, the chariot of the god Osiris, a sphinx, a veil lamp, Typhon the spirit of catastrophe, a lightning-struck tower, and other odd objects. Each of these things was part of an overall symbolism, adding up to an arcane knowledge that permitted the human will, working through actions and magically dominated inspirations, to overcome all obstacles to the achievement of divine wisdom.

If the applicant thought he was now through, the poor soul was badly mistaken. His terrors had scarcely begun. The guardian then took him into another room where they faced a blazing furnace.

"Son of Earth," the magus said, speaking loudly to be heard above the roar of the furnace, "if you are afraid, why did you come here? Death frightens only the imperfect. Look at me! Once I walked through these flames!"

The magus closed the door to the arcana, leaving the neophyte alone with the flames. The passage safely through the tunnel and pit had taught him that there is a way through these dangers. He had to be a highly intelligent person or he would never have been permitted to take the tests. He stepped forward, confident that he could meet and successfully challenge whatever the secret order had to give him.

As he came closer, he saw that the fires had been arranged in pots, which he had not been able to see before. These pots were so placed that there was a narrow passageway between the flames. By not showing fear and going ahead, he had opened up a way. But as he passed through the furnace, he came to a pool of water. Oil splashed down behind him, making a solid wall of fire. He was driven into the water, which got deeper as he advanced until he was up to his chin.

Then the floor of the pool began to rise. Ahead he could see a bronze door with a lion's head on it. A ring was in the lion's mouth. The ring, like the belt of the magus he met earlier, was in the form of a snake grasping its own tail. At this point the flames behind him died. He was left in pitch darkness. As an echoing voice warned him: "To stop is to die!" he plunged ahead through the water.

In the darkness he found the door and grasped the ring in the lion's mouth. He hoped that it was some kind of knocker that would summon the guardian of the door. But as he grabbed the ring, the floor fell from under him. He clung frantically to the ring to keep from falling into the darkness that cloaked whatever danger was below.

Then the trap under his feet closed again. The bronze door opened and the trembling man was taken inside. Twelve guardians of the sanctuary guided him down long corridors to a chamber hollowed out of stone. He was told that this was in the center of the Great Pyramid. (Current archaeology shows that this was not true.) The walls were covered with curious astrological and esoteric symbols and paintings.

The entire ruling group of the society awaited him in this room. The Master, clothed in purple with a gold circlet set with seven stars on his head, was surrounded by the others. They were dressed in white and stood in a semicircle around the Master. Behind the throne was a huge statue of Isis. There was a silver table in front of the Master. On it was a huge horoscope design.

The initiate was then given a horoscope to work out and explain to the assembled group. When he successfully completed this, the Master told him:

"One day you heard that we possess a store of supernatural knowledge. You knew no rest until you received permission to join us. All we ask of you, even if you wish to be restored to liberty, is your solemn oath that you will never reveal to anyone the least detail of what you have seen and heard this night. Will you take this oath?"

"I will," the applicant replied.

"We are witnesses to your oath. If ever you are guilty of perjury, an invisible vengeance will follow you in your ways. It will reach you wherever you may be. From this moment forward you are counted among the disciples of Wisdom, and you will bear, among us, the title of Zealot, until by great acts of obedience you earn the right to be raised to higher rank."

At this point the applicant thought he was finished at last. Instead the lights went out and there was the noise of a mighty storm. When this ended and he could see again, all the magi in the room encircled him with swords pointed at him. The Master offered him two goblets with these words:

"You have sworn an oath. But we want the gods themselves to guarantee your sincerity. One of these cups holds wine. The other is a deadly poison. Select one and drink!"

Some faltered at this point. They were not permitted to leave but were put in a prison cell with a copy of the *Book of Thoth* to study for seven months. Then they were again offered the two cups. This went on until they chose to drink. After that, they were given the lowest rank of Zealot, but could never rise higher.

According to magical tradition (without any direct evidence), Pythagoras and Plato both underwent these Egyptian initiations. Both accepted the cup without hesitation. There was no poison. It was all a test of the applicant's sincerity.

There is no particular reason to doubt Iamblicus' description of these magical initiations. However, the sole evidence that Plato and Pythagoras experienced them is indirect. After leaving Egypt, Pythagoras set up his own brotherhood welded into a secret society. Plato returned to Greece, after studying thirteen years in Egypt, and opened his famous academy. There is certainly nothing to show in his later life that he introduced any of the secret rites of magic into his teachings.

Much more has been written about a mysterious figure who lived just before and just after the time of Christ. Where Plato and Pythagoras were content to study just in Egypt, this man—the fabulous Apollonius of Tyana—sought magical wisdom in all of the great centers of his known world.

❖ 3 ❖

Apollonius of Tyana

All we know of the accomplishments of Apollonius of Tyana come to us secondhand. He—like Pythagoras—wrote nothing himself. His disciple, Damis, kept notes during his years with the master. Philostratus used these to write his famous biography of the mystic master. Thus we have the story of Apollonius filtered first through the worshipful eyes of a follower and then through still another somewhat credulous person before it comes down to us. Such people are all too often inclined to attribute magical reasons to perfectly natural phenomena. Actually, the really great magicians have always claimed that true magic is natural. It is just that its principles are beyond the comprehension of ordinary people.

This strange man called Apollonius is a godlike figure. Some have even claimed that his biographers have woven acts and attributes of Jesus Christ into the picture they have created of him.

His birth was fabulous. His mother was inspired by a dream to leave her home and go into the meadow where she went to sleep among the flowers. There Apollonius was born as swans flew down and awakened the woman by loudly flapping their wings. According to Philostratus:

> People of the country [that is, Tyana, a city in Asia Minor settled by Greeks] say that just at the moment of Apollonius' birth a thunderbolt seemed about to fall to earth and then rose up into the air and disappeared. The gods thereby indicated, I think, the great distinction to which the sage would attain. They thus hinted in advance how he should transcend all things upon earth and approach the gods.

As the boy grew older he studied under a Phoenician magician in Tarsus. Even though still in his teens, he had the instinctive ability to detect the sincere and the insincere. He quit this teacher and went to Aegae, where he studied under a Pythagorean master.

Apollonius was so pleased with this teacher, Euxenus, that he persuaded the elder Apollonius—he was named for his father—to provide a villa for the aged master to live out his days in comfort. But for himself, Apollonius renounced all earthly comforts.

"I will live like Pythagoras," he said.

He renounced meat and wine and became a vegetarian. He felt that animal flesh was unclean because of the belief—called transmigration—that human beings can be reincarnated as animals as well as humans in later rebirths.

He did not claim that wine, made from natural foods, was unclean. But he said that it darkened the "ether of his soul," making him less sensitive to what lesser men call the supernatural. He did not define or explain what the "ether of the soul" is. Some present-day thinking identifies it with the *akasha*. At one time scientific thought did not believe that light could travel through a vacuum. So, to explain how light travels from the sun, moon, and stars, scientists postulated an "ether"—an atomically thin substance that extended through all the universe. It was thought to be too minute to be detected, but material enough to permit light waves to use it as a medium for travel.

Akasha is explained in much the same terms. It is said to be an indetectable substance that permeates all creation. It has the ability—like a cosmic tape recorder —to receive and hold radiations reflected by human thought and life. Thus the akashic records provide a history of everything that has happened since the dawn of creation. Masters of magic or the occult who have the ability to tune in on this cosmic record have at their disposal a library of all the knowledge and thought that ever was.

It would appear from the life of Apollonius that he did have some measure of ability to tune in through "the ether of his mind" to the akashic records—if there be such.

He went barefooted, wearing a simple linen gown.

He did not cut either his hair or his beard. He was said to have the face of a kindly god and the majestic bearing of a king. He inherited much property when his father died, but gave it all away.

The Pythagoreans taught him that silence is the greatest of virtues. Pythagoras is supposed to have told his brotherhood that "subjugation of the tongue is the most difficult of all victories." Following this principle, Apollonius went for five years without speaking a word.

He still traveled, however, ever seeking to learn more about magic, and at the same time never losing an opportunity to help his fellow man. He became a doctor, and stories of his miraculous cures were spread far and wide. Then he came to a town hurt by a drought. The local merchants withheld their grain from the market to raise the price. Apollonius wrote them a note. In it he pointed out that the grain had come from the earth as a gift of the goddess to mankind. If the merchants continued to withhold it from the hungry people, then he—Apollonius—would pray to the earth goddess that the grain dealers no longer be permitted to walk upon the earth, which is the body of the goddess. Apollonius' reputation as a magician was so great that the merchants believed him. They rushed to open their granaries.

The sage continued to travel widely. At Antioch in Syria he performed strange rites at sunrise. They were rituals that could be done only by Pythagoreans who had kept silent for a number of years. In his notes, Damis did not reveal the nature of the rites.

Apollonius next went to Egypt to study under the Egyptian priests. From Egypt he went to Babylon and then to Persia, where he was initiated into the Zoroastrian fire worship rites. This was Aryan magic that went back to that practiced in central Asia before the Aryan migration.

From Persia Apollonius, Damis, and two companions walked through Afghanistan and the fabled Khyber Pass into India. The Hindus of India were also of Aryan stock. The Persian magi had suggested to Apollonius that he go to India, for the Brahmins (the Hindu priest caste) were the greatest of all magicians.

Through their magic the Brahmins saw Apollonius coming. His entire history was revealed to them and they sent a messenger to meet and welcome him to India. This guide first took the visitors to the enchanted hill of the Brahmins, but he insisted that only Apollonius could go in to meet the masters.

Sax Rohmer's paraphrase of Philostratus (in *The Romance of Sorcery)* says:

> Alone, then, Apollonius advanced to the stronghold of sorcery. The hill upon which the Brahmins dwelt was of about the same height as the Athenian Acropolis. Its summit was enveloped in a kind of mist, which wholly obscured the walls from view. Apollonius asserts that, ascending upon the southern side, he came upon a well

above the mouth of which there shimmered a deep blue light, which at noon ascended aloft, colored like a rainbow.

Hard by was a fiery crater, which sent up a *lead-colored* flame, though it emitted neither smoke nor smell. The well was called the Well of Testing and the fire the Fire of Pardon. Here, moreover, were two jars of black stone, respectively the Jar of the Rains and the Jar of the Winds.

The summit of this hill was locally regarded as the navel of the earth, and upon it fire was worshipped with mystic rites. This fire was derived from the sun, to which luminary a hymn was sung there each day at noon.

This reference to fire worship indicates that Apollonius visited India before the Hindu religion was firmed up into its present form. The original Vedic religion of the Hindus was based upon worship of natural gods, of which the sun was one. Apparently worship of fire as a symbol of the sun was the heart of the original Aryan theology, for we find it deeply embedded in the Persian worship of their ancient god Ahura-Mazda.

The Brahmin magicians welcomed Apollonius. Their master, Iarchas, showed himself to be quite familiar with Apollonius' entire life history. After they talked for some time on philosophic matter, the Indians retired for their regular worship, but invited Apollonius to accompany them and take part in the rites. The most noteworthy occurrence was that they sat down for these rites, but did not use either chairs or the floor. They set the staffs they carried in prepared holes on the floor and then floated in the air, holding to the upright staff with one hand to balance themselves.

This trick—and it is a trick—has survived the centuries. It later created a sensation in London in 1833 when performed as part of a stage magic show by a Chinese magician. Harry Houdini, the famous American conjuror and escape artist, wrote a history of magic in 1906. In it he claimed that the earliest record of the suspension trick was found in the writings of Ibn Batuta, who lived in the thirteenth century. Houdini, usually so accurate in matters pertaining to conjuring, missed this reference in Philostratus' life of Apollonius.

Later a king came to consult the sages. Apollonius was invited to remain for the audience. Iarchas said they would eat first.

> Four tripods immediately moved forward of their own volition! Upon them were cup-bearers of black brass, which resembled the figures of beautiful youths. And the earth magically strewed soft grass beneath them. Dried fruit, bread, and vegetables were served and set before the royal guest and Apollonius by these mysterious automata. . . . Vessels and goblets formed of enormous jewels were passed to the guests by the bronze cup-bearers. These contained a mixture of wine and water.

Rohmer commented that this account "afforded Apollonius' critics [and the critics of his biographer Phi-

A nineteenth century woodcut from the Harry Houdini collection in the Library of Congress shows an Indian performing the levitation trick that Apollonius saw in India almost two thousand years ago. This is now a standard stage magician's trick.

lostratus] with matter for ridicule," while others have ignored this portion of the story and sought to find truth in other sections. Actually, it could well have been accurate reporting. Stage magicians like Robert-Houdin, Compars Herrmann, and the Wizard of the North (John Anderson) used the identical Hindu methods. As for making grass grow for the king to sit on, Roger Bacon, the thirteenth-century British magician-scientist, turned a section of his garden into a sunny spot in dead winter for a similar royal banquet.

Also, "Sir John Mandeville," author of a book of travel in the twelfth century, told of a banquet in China where girls appeared out of nowhere, served him food, and then disappeared before his eyes. Marco Polo likewise mentioned some remarkable sights at a banquet he attended at the court of Kublai Khan in China. Rohmer mentioned a passage in Homer that speaks of tripods that "roll'd from place to place . . . self mov'd, obedient to the beck of gods."

Conjuring tricks they may have been, but in the light of magical history there is no reason to doubt that they happened.

Unfortunately, little is recorded about the long philosophical discourses Apollonius had with Iarchas. One that is recorded is their discussion about the nature of the cosmos. At this time the Greeks believed that all things were composed of four elements—water, air, earth, and fire. Iarchas told Apollonius that there was a fifth element the Greeks did not know about.

"This is the ether," the Indian said. "This we must

regard as the element of which the gods are made; for just as all mortal creatures inhale the air, so do immortal and divine natures inhale the ether."

At this point a student of magic remembers Apollonius' statement that wine dulled "the ether of his mind." Iarchas' statement might also be used as some support for the akashic belief that an etherlike substance fills all creation and can be tapped by the properly trained occult mind. This ether has no relation to the nineteenth-century concept of a universe-wide medium for light or the ether used as an anesthetic; it is an occult substance beyond the comprehension of ordinary minds.

Apollonius asked which of the elements was created first. Iarchas replied that they were all created simultaneously. "A living creature is not born by degrees," he replied.

From this Apollonius had a burst of inspiration. "Am I," he asked, "to consider the universe as a living creature?"

"Yes," replied Iarchas.

They also showed Apollonius a strange stone with magical properties. It was called the *pentarbe,* a word that was not defined. Iarchas was quoted as saying:

> "The largest specimen is of the size of a fingernail, and it is conceived in the hollow of the earth at a depth of four fathoms [twenty-four feet]; but it is endowed with such force that the earth swells and breaks open in many places where the stone is.
>
> "In the nighttime the stone glows like fire, for it is red and emits rays. If you look at it, it smites

with a thousand glints and gleams. And this light within it is a spirit of mysterious power, for it absorbs to itself everything in its neighborhood."

After demonstrating the magical powers of the *pentarbe*, Iarchas presented his guest with seven mystic rings, named for seven magic stars. Then Apollonius resumed his journey. He returned to Greece, then went to Ephesus, where he stopped a plague. He worked other miracles in Corinth and in Rome.

Nero was now emperor, and soon Apollonius was accused of defaming the mad monarch. The sage was taken before Tigellinus, Praetorian prefect of Rome, for his trial. A statement of charges against Apollonius appeared on a scroll which was handed to the judge. Tigellinus unrolled it, but as he started to read, the lines vanished from the parchment!

A superstitious man, he started in fear and told Apollonius to go. "You are too powerful to be controlled by me," he said.

As he was leaving, Apollonius passed a crowd bemoaning the death of a young girl. He stopped, touched her, and spoke a few words. It is said that he put life back into the corpse. Her rich family tried to press a bag of gold upon him. He refused and went his way.

He continued to travel through the known world of his time, always seeking more knowledge and always helping others. Strange and hard-to-believe stories are told of these years. Then in the time of the Roman emperor Domitian (81–96 A.D.) he was summoned back to Rome. Domitian imprisoned him for preaching against the Roman tyrant.

In the trial, Domitian lost his nerve and refused to condemn Apollonius. "I acquit you of the charges," the emperor said.

Apollonius thanked him and then charged the emperor with mistreatment of the people, the senate with corruption, and the army with cowardice. "Take my body," he said scornfully, "but my soul you cannot take. Nay, you cannot even take my body, since I tell you that I am not mortal!"

Then he vanished!—or so Philostratus would have us believe. In any event, he left Rome and went to Ephesus. One day he was making a speech when he suddenly stopped. He looked terrified. Then he suddenly cried, "Smite the tyrant!"

The crowd stared at him in amazement. Apollonius shook off the trance that seemed to have gripped him for several minutes. Then, speaking in a calm voice, he told the people, "The tyrant Domitian has just been slain, even now as I spoke to you!"

As it happened, the emperor had been assassinated in Rome, just as Apollonius had divined across the Mediterranean Sea. An assassin had plunged a dagger into the emperor's body. The blow was not instantly fatal. The emperor fought back, killing his assailant. Then he fell, weakened by the heavy flow of blood. His guard ran in, and, just as Apollonius in far-off Ephesus cried "Smite the tyrant," one of the guards put a spear into the hated emperor's body.

Damis' notes end here and nothing is definitely known of Apollonius' life after this point. Tradition says that he lived to be very old and was honored for his knowledge and goodness.

Unfortunately, accounts about men like Apollonius are not trustworthy. Their biographers, gullible men, wove fact and fancy together in such a way that we are not able at this later day to separate the truth from the fiction. What does come through is that Apollonius, in the tradition of the truly great magicians, sought knowledge for the benefit of mankind and not for any personal gain.

The situation is quite different with the next great magician we have to consider. There is plenty of evidence of his magical activities—too much in some cases. This evidence ranges from the hysterical condemnations of Gregory Nazianzen to the fervid adulations of Libanius. The subject of their hate and love was the Emperor Julian, a royal magician who undertook to banish Christianity from the Roman empire and return his people to the old gods of Greece. He believed fervently in magic, studied it avidly, and tried to make magic work.

❖ 4 ❖

The Emperor Magician:
Julian the Apostate

In the hills beyond Ephesus, the ancient city on what is now the Turkish side of the Aegean Sea, there was a secret cave. Here a group of people gathered to carry on magical rites that combined rituals from ancient Persia and Greece.

One day in A.D. 357, the magician Maximus agreed to take a young man named Julian to see the mystic ceremonies. This had to be done in the greatest secrecy. The young man was the cousin of the Christian emperor of Rome, Constantius, a bitter foe of pagan magic. Constantius looked upon Julian as a possible rival and would use the slightest excuse to put his cousin to death. Attending an anti-Christian ceremony would be an ample excuse to eliminate the young man.

When Constantine the Great, the first Christian emperor of Rome, died in A.D. 337, he divided the empire between his three sons. Constantius received the eastern section, with his capital in Constantinople (now Istanbul). The other two sons died fighting each other and the entire empire reverted to Constantius.

Constantine also left three half-brothers, whom Constantius had murdered as possible threats to himself. One of these was named Julius, who had four children. The oldest son was killed with his father. The only daughter was married to Constantius and then disappeared. The other two boys, Gallus, twelve, and Julian, six, were too small to kill. Constantius, for all his cruelty, drew the line at slaughtering children.

Julian was placed in the custody of an old eunuch named Mardonius who had orders to raise the boy in the Christian religion. Mardonius did his best. But later, after he learned how Constantius had killed his father and brother, Julian could not reconcile his cousin-emperor's professed Christianity with such cruelty.

When Julian was eleven Constantius thought it wise to remove the boy from the capital. Julian was sent to a remote castle where he was practically a prisoner. Fortunately for Julian, there was a Christian bishop nearby who had a library with many classical works. He permitted the boy to read the books. In this way Julian first learned of the gods of ancient Greece. They appealed to him more than Christianity, which he hated because the emperor believed in it.

He kept his views to himself, out of fear for his life. However, when the boy turned twenty, Constantius felt more secure on the throne and gave Julian more free-

The ruins of Ephesus, the biblical city in Asia Minor where both Apollonius and Julian the Apostate practiced magic

dom. He got permission to travel as a student. While he professed to be seeking philosophers, he was actually seeking magicians. He sought out one of the most famous, a man named Edesius, who was afraid to accept the emperor's cousin as a student. Edesius suggested that Julian find Maximus, who had been Edesius' best pupil.

Julian had difficulty finding Maximus. The magician was in hiding to escape the witch hunters of the Christian emperor. So Julian studied for a time with two other pupils of Edesius, but was confused by their conflicting views. Finally, he located Maximus in Ephesus.

This was one of the great cities of the time. Today it is remembered for its associations with St. Paul and for being the site of the Temple of Diana of the Ephesians, one of the seven wonders of the ancient world.

Julian studied under Maximus for a time. We are not told how this was done, since they were afraid to meet together. Probably it was done in the same manner as Libanius—who was Julian's teacher later on—said he and the future emperor worked. Julian paid a trusted man to attend Libanius' lectures and make notes. Later Julian studied these.

After some time Maximus agreed to accompany Julian to view secret rites carried on in a cave hidden in the hills beyond the Temple of Diana. These pagan rites were based upon a mixture of ancient Persian beliefs and rituals to the Greek sun god Helios. Both were tributes to the god of light, and the magical illumination in the cave was said to come from the gods themselves.

The worshipers gathered around a huge image of the Persian god Mithra, shown killing a bull. In Persian mythology, when Mithra killed the bull the blood flowed down to earth, creating all living things, both animal and vegetable.

Neophytes were initiated by standing in a pit. There was an iron grating over their heads upon which the sacrificial bull was tied. Its throat was cut and the blood poured down on the initiates. This washed away their impurities. This sacrificial blood symbolized the start of earth life from Mithra's original sacrifice and the rebirth of the initiates into a new life within the secret cult.

The records do not say if Julian personally underwent this baptism of blood. He did continue to study with Maximus for some time. Then he moved on, ever pursuing esoteric knowledge of pagan gods and magic.

While Julian was delighting in his secret studies, his brother Gallus—who had been spared along with Julian —came into Constantius' favor. He was made caesar, a position second to the emperor, and the heir of the childless ruler. He then became governor of a province. This he ruled as a tyrant and was suspected of plotting against Constantius. He was brought to Constantinople and murdered.

Not long after this Julian was summoned to Milan, Italy, where the emperor had temporarily moved his residence. Julian thought he would also be killed, but Constantius' queen interceded for him and he was banished to Greece. No one could have been more delighted. He threw himself into searching out all the surviving pagan cults that had escaped the vengeful Christians. At one time he was initiated into the secret Eleusian mysteries held in a sacred pagan grove outside Athens.

Then Constantius recalled him. Libanius tells us, "There being no way to decline the offer, Julian, with tears in his eyes, invoked the goddess [Athena], and having prayed to her to defend him, took his departure."

Constantius then married Julian to his daughter

(whom Julian looked upon as a spy for her father), and sent him to Gaul (France) to command the Roman occupation army there. The army was having trouble keeping order. Julian knew nothing of military science, and it is probable that Constantius expected the younger man to be killed. Julian however studied and became a very good soldier, winning important battles against the Gauls.

In between battles he lived in Paris, which was then almost entirely confined to the small island in the Seine River now known as the Ile de la Cité. Here he studied and acted as judge. Once when a soldier was accused of taking state money, Julian decided there was no real evidence against him.

"If a man can go free just by denying the charge, how can anyone be found guilty?" the angry prosecutor asked Julian.

"If a man can be found guilty just because he is charged, how can anyone be found innocent?" Julian retorted.

Such things, plus his great ability as a military leader, endeared Julian to the soldiers. This was to prove Julian's salvation, for Constantius had become uneasy about the growing strength of Julian's army in Gaul. Perhaps he recalled how the great Julius Caesar used his own victories in Gaul to make himself dictator in Rome.

Constantius ordered the best soldiers in the army in Gaul to return to Rome.This would leave Julian with only a small, poor force to face the vengeful Gauls.

The soldiers had found a home in Gaul, much like the occupation troops of any army. They did not want to go home. They rallied behind Julian, proclaiming him emperor.

Julian did not know what to do. If he accepted, he would have to lead his army against the Roman legions of the emperor. In his indecision, he turned to magic. In a vision he saw the spirit of the Roman empire in the form of a beautiful man. The spirit said, "I have presided over your destiny since the day of your birth. I have often spoken to you in your dreams. If you refuse the crown of the empire, my mission for you is ended. If you accept, I shall be your guide to the end of your life."

This vision made Julian recall other forecasts indicating that he would occupy the throne of the Roman empire. Maximus, his magic teacher, had told him this years before. Then when he first arrived in Gaul, the streets of a town he passed through were decorated with crowns made of leaves. The wind blew one from its fastening and it landed on Julian's head. In another case, a witchlike old woman called him "Emperor!"

These were signs that a believer in magic could not ignore. Julian gave in to the entreaties of his soldiers. He led them on a march through Europe into Greece, where more joined him and he was cheered as he marched toward Constantinople. As he neared the capital in the fall of A.D. 361, word came that Constantius had died on his way back from the Persian front.

Julian's advisers were afraid that the news of Con-

Julian, the emperor-magician, as shown on a Roman coin struck during his reign

stantius' death from a fever was a trick to throw them off guard. Libanius says, "But Julian sent for a book out of his trunk. He showed them certain written oracles that had been set down before word came of Constantius' death." These oracles, given before Julian left Paris, promised him victory without bloodshed.

Libanius went on to say, "Now that the oracles were fulfilled, and the land and the sea were subject to him . . . he burst into lamentation, and his tears dropped upon the prophecies."

One of his first decrees after becoming emperor was to affirm the promise he had made in Greece to restore the old gods as soon as he was on the throne. As a guarantee of his word, he stopped at Eleusis, where he had been initiated into the Eleusian mysteries, and went through a baptism in bull's blood to cleanse himself of his former baptism into Christianity.

Julian's bitter enemy Bishop Gregory Nazianzen (writing in his *First Invective Against the Emperor Julian)* cried:

> No sooner had he inherited the empire than he publicly professed his impiety, as if ashamed of having ever been a Christian, and on this account bearing a grudge against the Christians. The very first of his audacities, according to those who boast of his secret doings, with unhallowed blood he rids himself of his baptism. . . . With victims and with sacrifices he inaugurates his palace, using evil counsellors for an evil reign.

Libanius had a different story to tell. He claimed that Julian brought a return to true piety.

> Fines were paid by those who had used the materials from the [pagan] temples for their own houses. One might behold columns carried back to the plundered gods. . . . In all quarters were to be seen altars and fire and burning fat and smoke and ceremonies, and diviners released from fear. And on the tops of mountains were pipings, and processions, and the ox that sufficed at once for the worship of the gods and the banquet of men.

Julian's moral character, aside from his religious beliefs, was probably better than that of any other Roman emperor who ever lived. Even the bitter Gregory Nazianzen acknowledged that Julian was an able administrator. He was also a humble, democratic, highly moral man. He did not persecute the Christians as some former Roman emperors had done. This did not please Gregory. He railed at the emperor (after Julian was dead, of course) for not throwing Christians to the lions as Nero had done. In neither of his *Invectives* did Gregory ever refer to Julian by name. He refused to use a word he considered so foul. Julian was always referred to as "he" or "the emperor." Sometimes for variety Gregory might call Julian "this unhappy man."

Gregory explained his odd idea about persecution of his fellow Christians in this manner: "He begrudged the honor of martyrdom to our combatants. For this reason he contrived to use compulsion, and yet not seem to do so. That we might suffer, and yet not gain honor as through suffering for Christ's sake."

He admitted that "the government was administered with moderation, taxes were lowered, and wise judges appointed." But to Gregory these were only outward signs of prosperity, for paganism was sure to lead them all to hell.

Actually, in the light of history, Julian was a tolerant man. He restored the old gods and asked the people to follow them. No one was forced to do so, although he bribed the soldiers with a gold coin each to embrace the pagan religion. As for persecution of Christians, all he personally did was order those who had taken material from the pagan temples to bring it back, and he ordered that Christian teachers should be removed from the public schools. He also decreed that they could no longer call themselves Christians, but should be known as Galileans.

Later, when he continued to have trouble with them, Julian wrote a bitter treatise, *Against the Galileans.* There were troubles in Alexandria, in Antioch, and in Constantinople. Julian's patience was wearing thin. It is possible that if he had lived longer, he might in the end have persecuted more martyrs than Nero did.

Becoming emperor did not change Julian's attitude toward magic. One of his first acts was to summon Maximus, his old magic teacher, to come to him. Maximus turned out to be an outrageous flatterer of the emperor and so arrogant to all others that he was put to death after Julian died in battle.

Julian had a temple built inside his palace. He went there every morning to pray and to act as high priest in the sacrifices. He was fascinated by the sun and the stars. What he wrote about them gives clues to his paganism. This reverence existed long before he learned that Constantius had murdered his family—a fact that he did not learn until he was in his teens.

He wrote of this (in *Upon the Sovereign Sun):*

> From my earliest infancy I was possessed with a strange longing for the solar rays, so that when, as a boy, I cast my eyes upon the ethereal splendor,

my soul felt seized and carried up out of itself. [Curiously, this was also the feeling of another ruler who tried to change his people's religion into one worshiping the sun—the curious Egyptian Ikhnaton.] . . . Also at night whenever I walked out in clear weather, disregarding all else, I used to fix my eyes upon the beauty of the heavens. I was so entranced that I neither paid attention to what was said to me, nor took any notice of what was going on.

On this account . . . they even suspected me, long before my beard was grown, of practicing magic by means of heavenly bodies. And yet at that time no book on the subject had fallen into my hands. I was utterly ignorant of what occult science meant.

Julian's drive to restore the old gods suffered a setback in A.D. 362. The Parthians under King Sapor attacked the Roman frontier in Mesopotamia. Emperor for only slightly over two years, Julian rushed off to do battle.

He took Maximus, the magus, with him. At Antioch (in present Syria) he tried to reopen an oracle of Apollo which was earlier destroyed by the Christian Roman emperors. He and Maximus went to the site at night and made sacrifices to implore the god to return and resume his predictions of the future.

Later, after Julian died, his enemies claimed that the temple ruins were reopened after the emperor had them sealed again. Inside was found the disemboweled body of a young woman who had been killed in a human sacrifice. Others claimed that the young emperor sacrificed many small children in his frantic efforts to persuade Apollo to revive the oracle. Julian's supporters denied these charges.

At first Julian won easy victories. Then the enemy retreated, destroying everything in its path. Julian was without food for his troops. Then King Sapor launched a savage counterattack. At one point the Roman line faltered. Julian rushed to rally his troops. A spear struck him in the side. In his *Second Invective Against Julian,* Gregory claimed the blow was struck by a Persian spy who gained the king's confidence. Libanius, in his *Funeral Oration,* said that King Sapor offered a reward to the man who killed Julian, but that none came forward to claim it. Libanius claimed that it was really a Christian spy in the Roman ranks who killed the emperor.

In any event, Julian was severely wounded. He first tried to make light of his wound. He climbed back in the saddle and shouted that it was only a slight scratch. However, the blood was flowing so heavily that he fell from his horse.

He was carried back to his tent where he slept on a lion's skin placed over a mattress. His generals implored him to name a successor, for Julian had no sons. He refused. The army had made him emperor and now he left it to the army to pick the new ruler.

The last pagan emperor of the Roman empire died on July 26, 363. His successors were all Christians. The old gods died with Julian, a man who sincerely believed in them and in magic as the link between man and heaven.

❖ 5 ❖

The Scientific Magicians

In the beginning of human consciousness natural science and magic were the same. Both were simply the observation of things that occurred in the world of the observer. Then the Egyptian priests developed applied science. They adapted natural science to augment their magic. They used steam power to open temple doors, the optical principles of mirrors to reflect ghostly images upon steam clouds or smoke, and the clever arrangement of lighting effects to make themselves appear and disappear magically.

But in the Dark Ages, when learning and investigation were stifled, scientific investigation turned from a form of magic to pure witchcraft in the eyes of the religious authorities who sought to dominate men's minds in this low period of human history. Even so, there are always some minds that refuse to be stifled. Unfortunately, most of the accomplishments of such men come down to us from awed, superstitious writers to whom these early scientists were black magicians and devil worshipers.

Roger Bacon, however, a Franciscan friar who was born around A.D. 1214, left enough writings of his own to prove that he was a true scientist, although his magical reputation was created by a play, *The Honorable History of Friar Bacon and Friar Bungay*, first performed in 1594. Friar Bungay was a young man Bacon met while both were students at Oxford University.

The magical traditions claimed that Bacon produced music from invisible musicians to entertain King Henry II, that he could cause lightning and thunder in a clear sky, and that he could raise ghosts of famous people. Other accounts claimed he could magically turn one person into a hundred, float himself up the wall of a building, and walk under water. Still others claimed that he could foresee the future and could fly in the air.

It is easy to see why the superstitious would ascribe such magical accomplishments to a man like Bacon, for every one of these claims has some basis in fact.

Bacon was a primitive scientist. He clearly understood the Egyptian methods of conjuring. We find this in his own writing. Once he wrote: "There are men who create illusion by the rapidity of their hands' movements, by the assumption of various voices, by ingenious apparatus, or by means of confederates so that they show to men wonderful things that do not exist."

In his treatise *Miracles of Art, Nature and Magic*, he gives hints as to how "wonderful things that do not exist" may have been done. He may not have done these things himself, but the fact that he wrote about them prompted legend makers to make claims that resulted in Bacon's reputation as a magician. "Glasses and perspectives may be framed to make one thing appear many, one man an army, the sun and the moon to be as many as we please," he wrote.

This indicated that he knew more about optics and lenses than anyone else of his time. Lens attachments are available today that permit taking five or more multiple images of a person on a single piece of film. While it is doubtful that Bacon could have ground a complex lens like this, it would have been easy to arrange a cluster of simple (miniscus) lenses to form multiple images. While Athanasius Kircher, in 1646, is credited with inventing the magic lantern for projecting slides, the camera obsura, which uses a lens to project an image onto the wall of a darkened room, was described by Ibn al Haitam (Alhazen) two hundred years before Bacon. With the Moors in Spain, it is quite likely that Bacon—with his inquiring mind—had seen or heard of the famous Arab's writings. Such optical knowledge would have made the production of "ghosts" a simple thing indeed.

As for the lightning in a clear sky, we know that Bacon experimented with gunpowder, and even developed a method for producing a purer form of saltpeter, an ingredient of the explosive. The basis for the claims that he actually produced thunder and lightning rests upon his statement, "It is possible to achieve the making of thunder and lightning in the air; yea, with a greater advantage of horror than those that are produced by nature. A very competent quantity of matter rightly prepared (the bigness of one's thumb) will make the most hideous noise and sparkling." Since Bacon says "It is possible . . ." we assume from this that he must have carried out the experiment himself or witnessed it done.

Some of the other claims of his sorcery rest upon his predictions. These have been twisted in the telling to become superstitious accounts of things he supposedly did himself.

He claimed that boats would be made that would move without sail or rowers, that devices would be constructed to permit men to walk on the bottom of the sea, and that chariots "would move with an inestimable swiftness . . . this motion to be without the help of any living creature." He went on to say that it was possible "to make engines for flying, a man sitting therein," and "it is possible to invent an engine . . . whereby a man may ascend or descend any walls. . . ."

Bacon said that all these things had been done at an earlier time and could be reinvented. Be that as it may, in his statements he very accurately predicted the steamship, the diving bell or submarine, the automobile or locomotive, the airplane, and the elevator. He may well have based his claim upon tales of the prior invention of these wonders which filtered down to him from Greece, China, and Arabia. For example, Daedalus, the Greek, supposedly invented wings to escape from Minos of Crete. And Hero of Alexandria, modifying the old Egyptian trick of using steam pressure, made an engine that revolved at a rapid rate.

Bacon's experiments conflicted with his religion, and he was imprisoned in 1278 and forced to abandon his scientific work. At this time he made a statement that is the very heart of all true investigations of magic made by serious "occult scientists." Bacon said, "We must remember that there are many books commonly reputed to be magical, but which have no other fault than discovering the dignity of wisdom."

This statement agrees perfectly with the beliefs of many other sincere magicians later on who have told us that there is no supernatural; what we call the occult is just part of the natural world, but we lack the expanded mind necessary to perceive its true reality.

Spanning the last years of the fifteenth century and extending into the sixteenth, we have two remarkable men who did more than anyone else of their time to explore this natural world beyond the normal senses that Bacon told us about. These two men were Cornelius Henry Agrippa von Nettesheim and Philippus Theophrastus Bombastus von Hohenheim. Cornelius is known to magical history as Agrippa and Philippus is called Paracelsus.

Agrippa and Paracelsus were contemporaries. Both were considered to be sorcerers, but they never worked together. Each went his own way and both contributed to the legend of the man who sold his soul to the devil in exchange for unholy knowledge—a legend that reached its climax in the curious life of Johann Faust.

Born in Cologne, Germany, in 1486, Agrippa was seven years older than Paracelsus. He graduated from the University of Cologne when he was fourteen. He seems to have studied in a number of other universities, for he had been born with a hunger for knowledge. He was naturally led to magic by the spirit of the times. About twenty-five years before Agrippa's birth, Cosimo de Medici of Italy had secured fourteen Greek manuscripts that were supposedly the writings of Hermes Trismegistus. Thoth, the Egyptian god of magic whom the Greeks associated with their own Hermes, had been dropped. To get away from the pagan associations of Hermes with the old Greek gods, later followers claimed that Hermes Trismegistus had been a real philosopher. In 1464 Marsilio Ficino translated these Hermetic writings and proclaimed them to be the oldest of magical books. Agrippa was among the eager young men who studied the Hermetic writings. Later the book proved to be no older than the Neoplatonist period of post-Christian Alexandria, but this was not known until 150 years later.

In the years that followed, Agrippa lectured widely in universities all over Europe. His reputation for learning increased enormously. However, he seems to have been associated in some vague way with the army in Spain. He and some friends took part in an attack upon a castle or fort held by some rebellious peasants. Agrippa is credited with bringing about victory either by some war machines he invented or by some kind of magic.

Cornelius Agrippa had a profound understanding of magic. His book, *De occulta philosophia*, strongly influenced the study of magic for three hundred years.

In the manner of old comrades-in-arms, Agrippa and his friends who took part in the battle formed a secret society among themselves. Alchemy and magic were part of it, although the main purpose was for the members to look out for each other.

As he tended to put more faith in science than in religion, Agrippa came into increasing conflict with Church authorities. This caused him to return to Germany to see Trithemius of Sponheim, a famous abbot who was also a serious student of magic. Encouraged by Trithemius, Agrippa finished a book he had been writing for some time. This was finished in 1510 and circulated among his friends in manuscript. It was dedicated to Trithemius. Entitled *De occulta philosophia (On Occult Philosophy)*, it was an encyclopedia of magic.

This was not a book of rituals and magic formulae. Instead, Agrippa summed up the magical beliefs of the Renaissance period, which followed the Hermetic tradition. Agrippa divided creation into three worlds. At the top was the intellectual world of God and the angels. Then there was the celestial world of the stars. And finally, the elemental world of the earth and all things within it. God made His power felt through the angels of the top world and the stars of the middle world. In the same way that God's power descends through the worlds, the power of the true magician can ascend through the celestial sphere into the realm of the angels.

This was a time of religious disturbances. In October 1517 Martin Luther nailed his ninety-five theses to the church door at Wittenberg, Germany, throwing down the challenge that would split the Christian religion into Catholicism and Protestantism. Luther and Agrippa were not the only intellectuals dissatisfied with the religion of their day. Many turned to the occult, seeking answers they could not find in the churches of the time. They believed that there was a divine revelation that had been lost and that magic could lead them back to it. As a result, Agrippa's book was eagerly sought. Unpublished, it circulated in manuscript only. Those fortunate enough to borrow it hired scribes to help them make copies.

Although he scorned organized religion, Agrippa was careful not to attack the Catholic Church. He insisted that his views of magic were merely the way to lead men back to the Church. He showed his sincerity in attacking superstition. While living in Metz, he volunteered to defend an old woman accused of witchcraft. Agrippa's belief in magic was so well known that there were many who thought this was the equivalent of permitting the Devil himself to defend the old crone.

Agrippa did not believe in witchcraft, but he was careful not to admit this to the court, for he knew that the court did believe in it. He acted more like a modern lawyer. He argued over legal points, accused the witnesses of vagueness, and got them to contradict themselves on the stand. The judge then dismissed the charges.

In 1526 he published a curious book called *On the*

Vanity and the Uncertainty of the Arts and Sciences. This book contradicted most everything he had written or lectured about before. He denounced Hermetic writing and called the Jewish Cabala pure superstition. The Cabala is an esoteric system of interpretation that claims to tell the hidden meaning of the Bible. He did not denounce astrology, since he was often called to cast horoscopes for noble families who patronized him. But he did say that astrology is based upon the known planets and that if there were undiscovered ones then the system in use would produce false results.

Finally his masterwork, *On Occult Philosophy,* was published in 1530. It was somewhat revised from the original manuscript version, but did contradict the denunciations of magic he published in *On the Vanity, etc.* four years before. Various writers have suggested that he published the earlier book as insurance against Church condemnation.

As he aged, Agrippa became more caustic toward religion and lost his royal patrons, so that he was in want part of the time. His reputation as a magician grew more sinister in the public mind. Strange stories circulated about him. One told how he used his magic to cover up a murder committed by spirits from hell. As the story goes, Agrippa was staying at a hostel. A fellow guest had heard of the famous magician. This man waited until Agrippa was called away one day. Then the man searched the magician's room, seeking magical secrets.

In a manuscript Agrippa was writing, the intruder

found a magic phrase used to invoke devils. He whispered the words aloud to fix them in his mind. Instantly a devil appeared in response to the magical summons. The would-be magician did not know how to protect himself and the angry devil killed him.

Agrippa, who was having trouble with the local authorities anyway, was aghast to return home and find the strangled man in his room. But if magic got him into this frightening situation, then magic could get him out. He pronounced the magic words and the devil-spirit again appeared, angry as such vicious spirits always are at being disturbed by mortals they despise. Agrippa, however, was experienced in this sort of evocation. He knew how to draw a magic ring around himself for protection.

He commanded the devil-spirit to enter the body of the dead man. The murdered man got up from the floor. His expression was dull, but his eyes gleamed with the hellfire that animated him.

"Go to the town square," Agrippa ordered. "Walk around for the space of one turn [that is, one circuit of the square] and then let the body die after all have seen it walking."

The demon, since it had no choice, did as Agrippa ordered. Thus, the people saw the dead man walk and then drop over as if killed by heart failure.

Moralist writers are reluctant to permit people they consider rascals and heretics to get away with crime. So when Manuel del Rio retold this story a half century after Agrippa's death, he claimed that the townspeople were not taken in by the ruse. They saw the strangulation marks on the dead man's throat and connected them with Agrippa's magic. The magician hastily left town before the outraged people could burn him at the stake, or so del Rio would have us believe.

Actually, Agrippa was surprisingly free of official interference with his work. His royal patrons often cut off his pensions and he frequently had to move to different towns to escape local wrath, but neither Church nor secular authorities bothered him much. He was arrested once, but this was for libeling the queen. She had cut off his allowance and he got angry about it.

The secret society Agrippa formed in his youth was still active and had grown, since many of his students were added to the rolls. Some of these obtained influential positions in the courts of Europe. They protected their master until his death in 1535.

While Agrippa was honored for his learning and ability as a teacher of science and philosophy in addition to his magic, Paracelsus was considered a rogue in academic circles.

Paracelsus was born in Switzerland in 1493. His father was a German doctor who came from a family that had fought in the Crusades three hundred years before. Paracelsus became his father's apprentice, stirring the bubbling pots of medicine, selecting proper herbs, and rolling pills.

The boy left home when he was fourteen to take up the wandering life of a scholar. He traveled from school to school, never satisfied and always seeking something new. Later he wrote of these years, "I found that the medicine I was taught would not cure. All those who had written about healing did not know the truth and tried to teach what they did not know themselves. . . . So I had to look for a different approach to knowledge and healing."

He turned back to folk medicine and, as he grew older, began to attack his fellow doctors violently. He was a poor speaker and took to writing to put over his ideas. Unlike the scholars of his day, he refused to write in Latin. His books were written in the Germanic language of the people.

He was a pioneer in medical cleanliness and preached that nature could do more than any doctor in healing the sick and wounded. Doctors fought back at him. He was driven from town to town . He continued to rage against them and at this stage first started to call himself Paracelsus, after Aulus Celsus, who had produced an encyclopedia in the first century A.D. By adding *para* (over or above) to Celsus' name, Paracelsus proclaimed that his writings were greater than those of Aulus Celsus.

Like so many others before and after him, Paracelsus failed to find the truths he sought in the academic teachings of his time. He turned to magic. Just as Agrippa had done a few years before him, he turned to the famous magician Trithemius, abbot of Sponheim. Although Church authorities often condemned his work, Trithemius was highly regarded as a teacher of ethics and history in addition to his studies in the

Cabala and esoteric occultism. However, he did not let magic interfere with his religious beliefs. Magic must be used only for helping mankind. Any traffic with demons or devils was a sin beyond redemption in his eyes.

He taught Paracelsus the rudiments of magic and introduced him to *alchemy*. When chemistry was just beginning, most philosophers at one time or another dreamed of turning base metals into gold. We are told that Paracelsus was one of the few who succeeded.

A servant of Paracelsus left this story after his master died. One day the magus told him that they were low on money. The servant was sent to an apothecary to get a pound of mercury. Paracelsus mixed the mercury with a substance about the size of a large hazelnut he took from a paper to which it was fastened with red sealing wax. This substance was placed in a crucible, which was put on four bricks. The servant was ordered to heap red-hot coals about the container. Then coal dust was slowly added to keep the fire burning. A lid was placed on the crucible and it was entirely covered with coals.

After a time Paracelsus had the fire put out. The crucible was left standing for an hour. Then the magus said, "We will see what God has given us."

"I removed the lid [the servant reported]. The contents had turned solid. I said, 'It looks yellow like gold.'

" 'Yes, it will be gold,' my master said. 'Take it to the goldsmith.' "

This sounds like another fantastic tale, but it is possible that it is absolutely true—as far as the servant knew.

Years later Paracelsus wrote (in his *Greater Surgery Book*): "But after these come the gold-making tinctures transmuting metal. Thus one tincture [in its original sense this meant dye] colors metal. These discoveries have given rise to the idea that one substance can be transformed into another. . . . Such results I have attained in various kinds, always in connection with attempts to change metals into gold and silver."

It is close to impossible for Paracelsus to have colored a heavy metal well enough to fool a goldsmith. However, there are rascals in every trade. A dishonest goldsmith would have been delighted to buy at a good price colored metal that he in turn could palm off on unsuspecting customers as real gold.

Unlike so many alchemists who confined themselves to their smoky laboratories, Paracelsus—as he did in all matters concerning learning—went to the source for his information. Count Sigismund Fueger owned large mining properties in the Tyrol. Paracelsus went there and worked for some time in the count's metallurgy laboratory at the mouth of a copper mine. He learned how to use proper acids to dissolve ores and separate one metal from another. The count's copper was contained in iron ore. The ore was dissolved in vitriol and copper was precipitated out.

In writing about this, Paracelsus said, "It seems amazing that a metal should have the quality to disappear and turn into another. It is as strange as turning a man into a woman. . . . Therefore, in denying transmutation, Aristotle was foolish."

One of the most curious things that Paracelsus wrote

sounds as if he was a pioneer in growing what today is called a test-tube baby. He called it a homunculus. He gives only general instructions, saying that a sufficient quantity of the male human sperm should be collected in an alembic (a glass receptacle used by alchemists in distilling substances). This should be left for forty days to concentrate in a sealed container which has been buried in horse manure. The reason for placing the glass in the manure pile is that this material is supposed to maintain an even temperature.

Paracelsus goes on to say that if the sperm is properly magnetized—and he does not say how this is to be done—after forty days a living creature will start to form and move. It will resemble a human being, but will be transparent. This living substance is fed with *arcanum sanguinis hominis*. Arcanum means secret, but in this reference means elixir. So we have an elixir made of human blood. Again, the magus fails to leave us instructions about how to make this mysterious elixir. If this feeding is continued for forty weeks and the bottle left in the even temperature of the manure pile, the creature will grow into a human child. It will then look exactly like a human baby, except that it will be very small.

> We call such a being a homunculus [Paracelsus wrote]. He may be reared and educated like any other child until he is grown to his intellect and can take care of himself. . . . The art that gave this homunculus or little man life makes him one of the most extraordinary productions of human sci-

ence and the power of God. This little creature has intelligence. The mysterious manner of its birth gives it the ability to investigate and communicate to us the most secret mysteries.

Paracelsus' attacks upon both religion and medical doctors caused him to be barred from city after city. He was finally reduced to beggary. He clung, however, to a curious sword he always carried. It never left his possession, yet he never drew it in anger, for he was not a fighter. Even the woodcut made of him by August Hirschvogel shows Paracelsus clinging to the hilt of his sword. The top of the sword had a large knob that could be unscrewed to reveal an inner container. In this Paracelsus carried what he called his "elixir." On occasion he could be seen unscrewing the knob and taking out a pinch of some substance. This proved to be laudanum, a form of opium, which he learned about during a visit to Constantinople.

In his younger days Paracelsus made science his god. He bragged that he did not take erroneous knowledge from old books, but made his own experiments to prove what he learned. He taught that science could make men as great as God. To him science was mixed up with magic. Once he wrote: "The magus is neither from God nor from the Devil. He is of nature." Here he is echoing all the really great magicians who have told us that there is no supernatural. What seems like the occult is simply the natural which we still lack the training or ability to perceive.

Paracelsus holds the famous sword he always carried. His hand is on the knob that contained "secret elixir."

As time went by and he was reduced to rags and begging, he lost his faith in science and turned to religion. Although he now fervently embraced the Catholic Church, he just as loudly condemned its priests for corruption.

Henry M. Pachter (in *Magic into Science*) summed up this period of Paracelsus' life by saying that the magus tried to maintain the union of science and religion. "He tried the way of St. Thomas, that of the Cabala, and that of the mystics—and failed in each." From then on science and religion went different ways.

Then fortune changed. As a doctor, Paracelsus became fashionable again in the courts of Europe. However, he could not cure his wanderlust and kept moving, but he still found time to produce two major works. One was the *Great Surgery*, and the other was the *Great Astronomy or Sagacious Philosophy of the Great and Small World*. In this, his final book, he dealt with every scientific and occult subject that came to mind. He talked of sorcerers and witches, of fortune-telling by various means, healing powers of stones, the salvation of the human soul, the nature of the universe, and even made scientific predictions of the future.

In one part he spoke of magic that would carry the human voice "with the aid of pipes and crystals" over great distances. When he spoke of crystals, he seemed to be going beyond what became the telephone. Crystals were used in pioneer home radio sets, and today's fiber optics, just emerging from the laboratories, carries voices through "pipes and crystals."

He insisted that this and other marvels he predicted would come to pass through the magic of the Cabala—that is, through finding the esoteric truth behind the words of the Bible.

As his life drew to a close, he came under the protection of the bishop of Salzburg and ended his days by meditating on religion. He wrote his own epitaph:

Here lies buried
Philip Theophrastus
the famous doctor of medicine
who cured wounds, leprosy, gout, dropsy
and other incurable diseases of the body
with wonderful knowledge
and who gave his goods to be divided
and distributed among the poor.

He died on September 24, 1541, and is remembered as a peculiar man who earnestly tried to find the secret link between the world we know and the occult world we do not know.

❖ 6 ❖

The Soul Seller:
Johann Faust

Paracelsus and Agrippa were giants in the history of magic, but they are known mainly to students of magic. In the public mind, their fame is eclipsed by a strange half-real, half-literary person called Faust. Faust is the greatest personification of the knowledge-hungry man who goes so far as to sell his soul in his passion for the secrets of creation. Faust's reputation is based primarily upon legends and literary works, such as Christopher Marlowe's play *Faustus* and Gounod's opera *Faust*. These have firmly fixed in the public mind the picture of the man who sold his soul to the devil.

But like so much legend and mythology, there was a real Faust. He was a contemporary of Paracelsus and Agrippa. Some observers believe that aspects of these two great magicians have been incorporated in the Faust legends.

It is Trithemius, abbot of Sponheim, the old friend who taught Paracelsus and Agrippa their first magic, who first mentions the real Faust. Trithemius' opinion of Faust was not high. He wrote in a letter to a friend:

> That man about whom you wrote to me, Georgius Sabellicus, who has ventured to call himself the prince of necromancers, is a vagabond, an empty babbler and a knave. He is worthy to be whipped, that he might no longer profess abominable things which are opposed by the holy Church. He has adopted the following titles: Magister Georgius Sabellicus, Faustus junior, prince of necromancers, astrologer, chiromancer, aeromancer, pyromancer, and hydromancer. [This meant that Faustus junior claimed to tell fortunes by the stars, by palm reading, by the air, by fire, and by water.] The man is devoid of education and should call himself a fool, rather than a magus.

The abbot went on to say that once he was in the town of Gelnhauses. He heard of strange things being done by this man who called himself Faustus junior. The abbot asked to see the magus, but Faustus fled when told the abbot wanted to see him.

The abbot identified Faustus as George Sabellicus, with Faustus junior appended to the name. Later references by other writers dropped Sabellicus and junior, and referred to George Faust or Faustus. Then later he appeared as Johann Faust.

The references to Faust are numerous in correspon-

Trithemius of Sponheim studied magic in relation to religion. He was the teacher of Agrippa and Paracelsus, but he detested Faust.

dence preserved from the early sixteenth century. One refers to him as a palm reader and calls him a braggart and a fool. But the explorer Philip von Hutten says of his unfortunate expedition to Venezuela: "I must acknowledge that the philosopher Faustus divined it correctly, for we had a very bad year." In casting von Hutten's horoscope, Faust had advised against the expedition.

In another instance, an entry was found in the account books of the bishop of Bamberg listing payment to Doctor Faustus for casting the bishop's horoscope.

The patronage of the bishop and von Hutten would indicate that Faust was more highly regarded than Trithemius would have us believe. On the other hand, a Phillip Begardi wrote in 1539 that a man called Faust, who bragged of his magical accomplishments, was as famous as Theophrastus (Paracelsus). He added that despite the lofty promises made by Faust, his accomplishments were "small and fraudulent" and that he cheated many people.

A later account gave Faust's birthplace as Kundling, Germany. He later went to Krakow, Poland, where magic was taught in the university. He then took up the life of a wandering magician and fortune-teller. Trithemius said that at one time Faust was given the position of teacher at a boys' school, "but practiced a most infamous kind of fornication with the boys. He fled when the matter came to light."

Still later stories began to appear that tied Faust with the Devil. These stories had him signing a pact with Lucifer which guaranteed him twenty-four years of the Devil's aid, after which his soul was forfeited. It was also said that the Devil in the form of a black dog always traveled with Faust. This is probably a confusion of Faust and Agrippa. In his last years Cornelius

Agrippa did travel with a black dog. It was said of Agrippa that his last act before his death was to remove a collar carved with magical symbols from the dog's neck, saying, "Begone! You have been the ruination of me, you devil!" Whereupon the dog gave a hideous howl and vanished as Agrippa died.

These references to Faust are tantalizingly brief. All we get is a sentence here, a complaint there, and an occasional paragraph. It adds up to very little. However, the wide spread of these references shows that Faust was known in all levels of society. The exact date of his death is not known, but was between 1540 and 1548. He was not quickly forgotten like most mountebanks. His fame grew as his real accomplishments were embroidered into folklore.

In 1587 a small book called *Dr. Johann Faust, Notorious Magician and Necromancer* (English translation of German) was published in Germany. It was so popular that it was followed by forged books that claimed to be Faust's own magical secrets.

The original book was quickly translated into English under the title *The History of the Damnable Life and Deserved Death of Doctor John Faust*. This was the book used as source material by Christopher Marlowe for his play *The Tragical History of Doctor Faustus*. This is the play that contains the famous lines about Helen of Troy:

Was this the face that launch'd a thousand ships,
And burnt the topless towers of Ilium?

This etching by Rembrandt is reputed to be a portrait of Faust as
an alchemist.

These lines are spoken by Faust in the play when Mephistopheles brings the spirit of Helen to be Faust's earthly lover.

The English edition of the German book was published in 1588 and a second edition appeared in 1592. Both were passed by church censors because they were moral documents, despite being tales of blasphemy. They showed the terrors of hell and the vengeance that falls upon those who bargain with the Devil. Theologians looked upon the story of Faust as a grim warning to sinners and would-be dabblers in the forbidden arts.

According to this book, Faust's father was too poor to support his son. The boy was taken in by an uncle who wanted to train him for the ministry. "But he gave himself secretly to study Necromancy and Conjuration," the history tells us. He received his Doctor of Divinity degree, and then became very morose. He "threw the Scriptures from himself . . . and began an ungodly life."

He studied the books of the Chaldeans, Persians, Hebrews, Arabians, and Greeks. "He used figures, characters, incantations, with many ceremonies belonging to the infernal Arts, as Necromancy, Charms, Witchcraft, and Enchantments. Being delighted in these ancient books, and names, he studied day and night. . . . Without doubt he was passing wise, but he cared not for his soul. He regarded more for worldly pleasure than for the joys of Heaven to come. Therefore at the day of judgment there is no hope for his redemption."

Through his black arts, Faust was able to call up Mephistopheles, a spirit of Lucifer. He wanted the spirit as his slave "to be obedient to me in all things from this hour to the hour of my death."

Mephistopheles explained that he had no power himself. All his power came from Lucifer, the Devil. Although Lucifer had been expelled from Heaven, he still possessed great power and commanded legions of demons. The power of these, at the Devil's command, could be infinite. However, Mephistopheles explained, no demon is permitted to assist mankind unless the seeker "promises to be ours."

"I will not be damned!" Faust cried.

But Faust weakened. At their next meeting he agreed to give up his soul. A contract was written. The first articles specified that Mephistopheles would come at Faust's command and serve his master in all things that Faust required. Faust, in turn, was required to fulfill these obligations:

1. He should give himself to Lucifer body and soul.

2. He must confirm this agreement in writing, using his own blood for ink.

3. He must thenceforth be an enemy to all Christian people.

4. He must deny his Christian belief.

5. He must not listen to any who would change his belief in the devil.

6. In return for this agreement written in blood, Faust was promised whatever his heart desired for a

space of twenty-four years. At the end of this time, the Devil would claim Faust's soul.

His mind inflamed by the possibilities of the Devil's aid, Faust agreed eagerly to these conditions.

In the beginning, Faust was greatly interested in hell. He kept questioning Mephistopheles about the infernal place, for he was already beginning to worry about his future damnation. In the meantime, he lived a life of utter luxury with his every wish but one satisfied instantly. The denied wish was to marry. Mephistopheles was furious at the idea. He angrily told Faust that marriage was of God. In his contract, written in blood, Faust had agreed to forgo all the things of God. When Faust persisted in his demands, the Devil himself appeared in a blaze of fire to threaten Faust with instant death and damnation.

Faust trembled with fear. Mephistopheles told him, "We saw in your heart how you despised thy degree in Divinity, and how you sought to know the secrets of our infernal kingdom. Then we entered into you, giving foul and filthy suggestions, giving you a push forward and persuading you that your desire for knowledge could never be attained without the help of some devil."

"Woe is me!" Faust cried. "Had I not desired to know so much I would not be in this awful situation. I thought myself unworthy to be called Dr. Faustus, if I should not also know the secrets of hell."

Later, his worry dimmed by his hunger to know occult secrets, Faust forgot his fear. He kept urging Mephistopheles to reveal more to him. He complained that the ancient books of magic he read were confusing. The writers contradicted each other, and when he tried to follow their reasoning and directions he was lost. In this statement Faust was echoing the complaint of all of us who have tried to read books of magic.

Mephistopheles replied that these ancient writers had done nothing really. "If by chance some have left behind anything worthy, the knowledge has been so blinded with enigmatical words and obscure figures that it is impossible for an earthly man to understand what has been written. He will need aid of some spirit. We spirits know this. We know all things, except the date of the Time of Doom."

The infernal spirit went on to say that he would teach Faust the courses of the planets, the way of the sun, the nature of the elements (that is, fire, water, air, and earth), and how to make thunder, lightning, hail, snow, and rain. He promised to show Faust how to make earthquakes that would split rocky cliffs and how to make the sea rage and roar.

He told the entranced magus that he would be able to fly as Mephistopheles flew, to have the love of the most beautiful women be they alive or dead, and to walk through doors, walls, and gates of iron.

Whatever else may be said of the Devil, he keeps his promises. Faust was able to do all these things. With Mephistopheles carrying him, Faust flew to all countries of the world. He was taken even into hell, and given a distant view of paradise. They flew near the sun. Faust later wrote to a friend that although the sun appears small from the earth, "it is altogether as big as the world." The heat on this flight was so great that Faust would have burned to a cinder if Mephistopheles had not thrown a shadow over him.

Faust learned the secrets of the universe. He was astonished to find that the sun was stationary and that the planets revolved around it. Here in this passage, the unknown author of the Faust history took the ideas of Copernicus, who was a contemporary of Faust, Agrippa, and Paracelsus. In this manner he was writing science fiction, according to the latest scientific thought of his day.

Faust also learned how God had made man through the use of the four elements—fire, water, earth, and wind. There was darkness and God made light, which is fire. Then Adam was molded of clay—the earth. "The earth will shape no image without water," Mephistopheles said. So the clay was wetted with the second element. Then God breathed life into the nostrils of the clay image—and this was the first wind.

Throughout the book, although it is an account of Faust's wickedness, the damned man always comes back to the wonders of God. He would fall into despair and cry, "Woe is me! My haughty mind, my aspiring stomach, and filthy flesh have brought my soul to eternal damnation!"

At one point Faust asked Mephistopheles what he would have done if he had been in Faust's place. The answer, from a devil, is surprising. Mephistopheles replied that if he had been a man with Faust's ability and mind, he would have humbled himself before God, so that he could have ensured for himself eternal joy in the Kingdom of Heaven.

As the book continues, the writer seems to have run out of new wickedness and wonders to describe. Faust degenerates into a common trickster, using his magic powers to amuse and tease. He consorts with princes and kings, astounding them with his magic tricks. In one case, he saw a drunken knight sticking his head out of a window. He conjured a set of huge antlers to the man's head so he could not draw back into the room. In another case, Faust was annoyed by the noise of some loud-mouthed students at an inn where he put up for the night. He froze them all with their mouths open until he got ready to leave.

Once Faust was the guest of the duke of Anholt. He noticed that the duchess was expecting a child. Knowing that pregnant women often have a longing for odd or out-of-season fruits, he asked the duchess what she craved. She said she longed for grapes and fresh fruits. Since this was winter, there were none to be had.

"Gracious lady, that is a small thing to do," Faust said.

He took a plate from the table and walked to a window. He pushed it open and held the plate out into the dark night. When he brought it in again, the plate was heaped with grapes, apples, and pears.

The duke wanted to know how Faust accomplished this miracle. Faust explained that only half the world is in winter, the other half being in summer at the same time. In this summery portion of the world fresh fruits were growing. It was a simple matter to have his spirit, which traveled in the flash of an eye, bring what the duchess desired.

Faust then felt an obligation to return the duke's hospitality. An enormous castle quickly appeared on a barren hill. Faust invited the duke and duchess to dine with him there. As they entered, they saw the moat filled with waterfowl, many from tropical climes never before seen in Germany. Stranger wonders filled the courtyard. It was crowded with tame beasts of every kind. Apes, bears, antelopes, and others moved together in peace. The meal in the great dining hall was the most magnificent ever served. There were nine kinds of meat, and wine from every country in the world. Later, as the duke and duchess returned to their own castle, they saw the magic castle of Faust disappear in thunderous fire. The noise was so loud that it seemed that giant cannon were firing.

As Faust grew old and close to the end of his allotted twenty-four years, he turned more and more to students, teaching them and making merry in their company.

One night as the wine flowed freely, the talk turned to beautiful women. One student claimed that Helen of Troy must have been the most beautiful of all women, for the Greeks and Trojans dared so much for her. Another said that he wanted more than anything else to see Helen.

Faust replied that he had once brought back Alexander the Great for King Carolus (ruler of a small German state) to see. So could he show them Helen, the fairest woman of ancient Greece, as she looked at her most radiant time. He did so and the students were captivated. They begged Faust to bring her back the second night, but he refused. Perhaps this was because he had fallen in love with the beautiful spirit himself. In any event, in the twenty-third year of his agreement with the Devil, Faust brought back Helen to be his lover. They had a child whom they named Justus.

As the twenty-fourth year drew to a close, Mephistopheles brought back the document written in Faust's blood. He warned the agitated magus to prepare himself for the payment of his bargain. Faust wept and bemoaned his fate, but could do nothing about it.

On the last night he called his friends together. He told them of his pact with the Devil, and that now he had to pay with both his body and soul. The students begged him to turn to God, but Faust replied sadly that it was too late.

He went to his room in the inn. About midnight a terrible storm struck the town. Hideous noises were heard in Faust's room. The next morning the students went to the room and found it splattered with blood. Faust's battered body was found thrown in the horse lot. Helen and their son Justus disappeared. They were never seen again.

Marlowe's play, which was based upon this story, was extremely popular, but gave a shallow interpretation of Faust's character. It inspired many lesser plays and stories.

Oddly enough, it was Marlowe's play that kept the Faust legend alive in Germany. British acting companies took the play to Germany, beginning in 1608. Later the play was translated into German. This in turn was corrupted into various versions and even made into a highly popular puppet play. These kept the Faust legend alive through the seventeenth and eighteenth centuries. The climax came when Johann Wolfgang von Goethe (1749–1842) saw one of these puppet plays. This inspired him to write his poetical version of the legend, which is considered to be one of the supreme achievements of literature.

After several earlier attempts, Goethe published *Faust, Part One of the Tragedy*, in 1808. This somewhat distorts the original Faust story. There is a prologue in which God and the Devil make a wager on whether or not Lucifer can corrupt the devout Faust. The Devil, through Mephistopheles, approaches Faust, an aged scholar who has been unable to satisfy through religion and magic his enormous hunger for knowledge. Faust does not sell his soul, as in the other versions of the story. He wagers with the Devil that he cannot be provided a moment of life so wonderful that he would want it to last longer.

Mephistopheles restores Faust's lost youth. Faust falls in love with Margarete and kills her brother in a duel. He abandons the girl and goes off with Mephistopheles to a witches' sabbat—a midnight assembly. Then, learning that Margarete has been condemned for killing the child she had by Faust, the magus comes back to save her. She refuses, claiming she has sinned and must pay for her sin. In this way she can receive atonement. As she dies, a voice from Heaven announces her salvation.

When presented on the modern stage as a verse drama, *Faust* usually ends here at the conclusion of Part One. However, Goethe continued to work on the play, publishing the second part in 1833. Here Faust is shown as he continues through his allotted years, including his marriage with the spirit of Helen of Troy and the birth of their son. When the boy dies fighting for the liberation of Greece, Helen returns to her spirit world. Finally developing a sense of responsibility to his fellow man, Faust reclaims land from the sea to help the poor. Through this action he redeems his soul and is reunited in death with the spirit of Margarete.

Charles Gounod, the French composer, used the first part of Goethe's verse as the basis of his opera *Faust*. It varies somewhat from the basic plot, however. Mephistopheles (a bass singer) tempts Faust (a tenor) with the sight of Marguerite (a soprano—the spelling is Gounod's) and promises the aged scholar both the girl and his lost youth if he will sign away his soul. This goes back to the original legend instead of using Goethe's wager. From this point, the opera generally follows the plot outline of Goethe's *Faust, Part One of the Tragedy*. It ends with Marguerite dying in prison as a chorus of angels sings of her salvation.

Literally hundreds of authors and composers have been inspired by the Faust legend. After Goethe, Heinrich Heine and Thomas Mann are the most famous.

From the composers inspired by Faust we have such famous works as Richard Wagner's *Faust Overture* (1840), Louis Hector Berlioz's *Damnation of Faust* (1846), the *Faust Symphony* (1861) by Franz Liszt, and *Doktor Faust* (1925) by Feruccio Busoni.

It is curious that a man so little regarded in his time, denounced constantly as a fraud and rascal, should have grown into such a tremendous literary and musical character.

It is almost as if magic were involved.

❖ 7 ❖

The Queen's Sorcerer:
John Dee

On May 28, 1555, the Privy Council of Her Most Catholic Majesty, Mary, Queen of England, issued an order "to make search for one John Dee. Apprehend him and send him hither, and make search for such papers and books as may touch upon the same John Dee."

The charge against Dee was the most serious it was possible to bring in the England of his day. He was suspected of using magic and sorcery against the life of the queen.

These were extremely suspicious and disturbed times in England. Henry VIII had broken with the Catholic Church because of the pope's refusal to grant him a divorce. Henry then established the Church of England with himself as the titular head. Lands belonging to the

Catholic churches were confiscated, and Catholics in general were put in a difficult position.

Henry died and was succeeded by his sickly son, Edward VI. Edward died in 1553, and the throne went to Henry's eldest daughter, Mary. Mary was a Catholic. Worse, she was married to Philip II, king of Spain and an ardent supporter of Catholicism. Those who supported Henry's break with the Church were now in an extremely difficult position as Protestants under a Catholic ruler.

The Protestants were not strong enough to risk a war with Spain by a violent overthrow of Mary. However, they were secretly looking for some way to depose her and place her Protestant half-sister Elizabeth on the throne. John Dee's arrest was ordered because informers told the Privy Council that Dee was using sorcery against the queen in support of Elizabeth.

At this time Dee was on his way to becoming one of the most learned Englishmen of his time. After studying in Belgium and Paris, he returned to London during the last three years of Edward's reign. Friends introduced him at court, and he became tutor to the children of important people.

When Edward died, Dee's fame was so great that Mary selected him to cast horoscopes for herself and her royal husband in Spain. Mary realized the grave situation that confronted her as Catholic queen of a Protestant country. She wanted some indication of what to expect during her reign. Dee was reassuring.

He told the new queen that the stars foretold a peaceful reign for her.

Two years after this an informer told the Privy Council, comprised of the queen's top ministers, that Dee had cast the horoscope of young Princess Elizabeth, Mary's half-sister and next in the line of succession to the throne. He compared her horoscope with that of Queen Mary and told Elizabeth that she would one day be queen herself.

The suspicious council saw this as a possible threat to the queen's life, believing that the evil Protestants might be using magic against Mary. The council did not want to bring the queen's name into any public accusation against Dee. So he was charged only with being a "conjuror, a caller of devils, a great doer of magic, and the arch villain of this whole kingdom."

Dee charged that this was a black plot by his enemies. Every word of the accusation, he claimed, was a "damnable slander, utterly untrue, on the whole in every part and word thereof."

Dee had many friends who stood up for him. The evidence that he tried to destroy the queen with enchantments was too flimsy to sustain a conviction. He was released, but immediately rearrested and sent to the bishop of London for a new trial. This was to determine if his sorcery was an affront to God.

Dee surprised everyone by persuading the bishop of his innocence. Sax Rohmer (in *The Romance of Sorcery*) says, "Considering Dee's reputation, the beliefs and superstitions of the times, and the fierce bigotry of his judge, I regard it as one of the most notable points in Dee's life that he convinced the Bishop of the orthodoxy of his faith. Probably no man ever came nearer to a Smithfield stake and escaped the burning." Smithfield was where sorcerers and witches were burned in pre-Elizabethan England.

In the tradition of the great serious magicians, John Dee had a passion for knowledge. He was born in 1527, the son of a master of the kitchen to Henry VIII. He entered St. John's College at Cambridge. Here "in the years 1543, 1544, 1545, I was so vehemently bent to study, that for those years I did inviolably keep this order," Dee wrote later. "Only to sleep four hours every night; to allow to meat and drink—and some refreshing thereafter—two hours every day; and of the other 18 hours all (except the time of going to and from and being at divine services) was spent in my studies and learning."

After his three years at St. John's, Dee became under-reader in Greek at the new Trinity College, also at Cambridge. While here he produced Aristophanes' play *Peace* in Greek. As part of the play a giant beetle flies down with a man on its back. Dee constructed a mechanical device to reproduce the insect's flight. This had been done in ancient Greece, but apparently it was the first time such a machine had been seen on the English stage. Dee tells us that there were "great wonderings and many vain reports" as to how he accomplished the wonder. The wondering was among the intellectuals of Cambridge. But when word of the flying mechanical insect reached the common people, they did not wonder about how it was done. They thought they knew: it was magic. This was the beginning of the dark rumors that Dee was in league with the Devil, which would cause him trouble in the years to come.

After two years at Trinity College, Dee turned down an invitation to lecture at Oxford and went to Europe to continue his studies. He had already begun to study alchemy, Hermetic magic, and the Jewish Cabala, and went to Louvain in Belgium because Agrippa had taught there twenty years before. Before returning to England in 1551, Dee lectured on Hermetic magic and mathematics in Paris, drawing excited crowds and adding to his personal fame.

After his return to England, Dee was arrested in 1555 for predicting that Princess Elizabeth would one day be queen. He narrowly escaped prison, if not death at the stake, because of this, and kept quiet until Mary's death in 1558. Elizabeth, the new queen, had not forgotten her favorite astrologer. She refused to be crowned until John Dee personally cast another horoscope for her and picked an auspicious day for the beginning of her reign.

He must have done a good job, for the Elizabethan Age was a golden period for England. Dee was not only a good astrologer, but was among the foremost scholars of the time. He had an international reputation as a mathematician.

He was a friend and student of the geographer Gerald Mercator, whose "Mercator's Projection" was a

John Dee, friend of Elizabeth I, was one of the most learned men of his time and an ardent student of magic.

new and practical method of drawing flat maps of the round surface of the world. Dee's own reputation as a geographer was also considerable. He was often consulted by the greatest explorers. He advised Martin Frobisher, whose expedition brought the first Eskimo back to England. Dee also appears to have been involved in some of the initial planning of Sir Francis Drake's voyage around the world.

Later Dee was involved in Sir Humphrey Gilbert's attempt in 1580 to explore parts of Canada. Dee was promised large tracts of land in the areas to be explored. Unfortunately, the expedition was shipwrecked and Gilbert was drowned. Then three years later Dee worked with Adrian Gilbert and John Davis on a scheme to colonize "Atlantis," as Dee called America. Gilbert was Sir Humphrey's brother and the half-brother of Sir Walter Raleigh. Nothing came of this venture, and Dee later became so involved with the arch-rascal Edward Kelley's attempts to make gold that he abandoned geography entirely.

Dee also owned the largest library in England. Earlier, he tried to get Queen Mary to establish a national library. When she refused, Dee set out to build his own. He beggared himself to buy books and manuscripts, and to have copied those he could not buy. He often spent his last cent for a new manuscript. When he found one he was happier than if he had been given a crown. In 1563 he wrote an excited letter to William Cecil, a friend, saying that during his stay in Antwerp he had been able to obtain a copy of Trithemius' *Steganographia*. This book by the abbot of Sponheim, friend to Agrippa and Paracelsus, was not published until 1606, but was circulating in manuscript.

Dee wrote that men had offered a thousand crowns (a silver coin then worth five shillings) for the manuscript without being able to obtain it. He does not say how much he paid to have it copied. His purchase of the *Steganographia* is significant, for it was from these writings of the magician-bishop of Sponheim that Dee learned about angel magic.

Dee was referring to this manuscript when he wrote that he had been unable to find the truths he sought in books and studies and had turned to prayer to the Giver of Wisdom "to send me such wisdom, as I might know the natures of His creatures. . . ."

In his book Trithemius taught that different groups of angels governed different parts of the earth, and his manuscript dealt with how to summon these angels. This is much the same thing that black magicians were doing with demons, but Trithemius, being a pious man, would have no truck with Satan's children. He sought the same magical association with God's angels. In his calculations for angel magic, Trithemius got deeply involved in astrology and numerology, which may have been based upon the number magic of the Pythagoreans.

Agrippa and Paracelsus had the advantage of receiving instructions directly from Trithemius. Dee, unfortunately, had to rely on manuscripts, for Trithemius was long since dead. This was not an entirely satisfactory way to learn. While he pointed Dee in the direction to go, the real secrets of angel magic were not revealed. Trithemius did not put all he knew into his writings. When Agrippa sent his old teacher a copy of *De occulta philosophia,* Trithemius evidently thought his pupil had told too much. He wrote Agrippa, "Yet this one rule I advise you to observe, that you communicate vulgar secrets to vulgar friends, but higher and secret to higher and secret friends only."

This was the policy of most ancient investigators of magic. Magic was too dangerous to be placed in the hands of just anyone. It could be written about in general terms only, with deeper secrets disguised so that only the initiated could understand them. This is the basic idea of the Cabala, which is supposedly the key to hidden secrets in the Bible. Such keys to the arcane in the writings of the great magic masters were communicated to their pupils in oral instruction and never committed to writing. The legend of the sorcerer's apprentice, who got into trouble for trying to work spells, and the story of the man who was killed by the demon he evoked after stealing an incantation from Agrippa are examples of the horror stories told to support the need for keeping the fundamental aspects of magic a closely guarded secret. This is why it is so difficult to judge the exact knowledge of these old magicians; they have not left us a record of all they knew.

After he received Trithemius' manuscript, Dee turned more and more away from science to magic as a source of knowledge. At the same time, his enormous extravagance in buying old manuscripts created a pressing need for money, which he hoped to get through alchemy. This led Dee into his association with Edward Kelley, one of the great rascals of magic.

Kelley (whose name is sometimes spelled Kelly) appears to have been named Talbot when he was born in 1555. His early life is obscure, but there are claims that he learned chemistry in an apothecary shop and later became a lawyer. He was especially skilled in penmanship. He then studied ancient Welsh and archaic writing and turned to forging land deeds. He was caught and punished by having both ears cut off. Thereafter he wore a black skullcap that came down over the sides of his face to hide his mutilation. This gave him a rather sinister look that fitted well with his future profession of alchemist and magician.

One night while stopping at an inn in Glastonbury, Kelley was talking to the innkeeper about the local abbey, which was founded by St. Dunstan (A.D. 925–988), later archbishop of Canterbury. A number of famous people had been buried at the abbey. St. Dunstan, like Trithemius, was reputed to have dabbled in a religiously accepted form of magic.

The innkeeper told Kelley that two men had broken into a sepulcher at the abbey, looking for gold they thought had been buried with a bishop. All they found was a manuscript written in a language they could not read and two small ivory caskets. One contained a red powder. The other was filled with a white powder. The casket containing the red powder was broken and much of its contents lost. Unable to see any value in these articles, the thieves traded the manuscript and the containers of powders to the innkeeper for a skin of wine.

Kelley recognized the powders as alchemical substances and the manuscript as the long-lost *Book of St. Dunstan*, which contained the secrets of the archbishop magician. He concealed his excitement, telling the innkeeper that the powders and book were of no value. He finally let the man talk him into taking them for five pounds.

Kelley rushed off to London with his treasures. He contrived to meet John Dee, but Dee was more interested in Kelley as a scryer—crystal gazer—than as an alchemist at this time. Dee claimed that the angel Uriel had given a polished black stone to him. An adept scryer could see the future in it. Dee tried, but the best he could see were blurred images. Kelley claimed to be an expert scryer, and Dee welcomed him.

In crystal gazing, the scryer does not actually see images in the glass. The ball acts as a point of focus to narrow the attention of the crystal gazer. This causes him or her to cut out all extraneous thoughts, emptying the mind in a kind of self-hypnosis. Thus the crystal gazer can concentrate entirely upon the secrets of the future. This leaves the mind uncluttered by other thoughts and receptive to receiving occult vibrations which create mental pictures or ideas, as the case may be, in the crystal gazer's mind.

Dee was delighted with Kelley's work as a scryer. From this they progressed into Trithemius' angel magic, and then into alchemy as Dee's fortune was spent. St. Dunstan, like most magical writers, did not tell all he knew about making gold from base metal.

Dee and Kelley had to do much experimenting, which was extremely costly. In the end Kelley supposedly produced gold, but he did so at a tremendous expense to Dee.

A difficulty the two alchemists faced was that there was but a small amount of the essential red powder in the broken casket taken from the desecrated grave in the abbey. St. Dunstan's book gave no instructions on how to make more. At this point in their experiments Count Albert Laski, a Polish nobleman, came to England on a diplomatic mission. He wanted to see Dee, and Queen Elizabeth arranged the meeting. Laski was so impressed with Dee and Kelley that he invited them to return with him to Poland.

They almost bankrupted Laski in their mad search for the secret of making gold. During this time, Dee received word from England that local peasants, inflamed by stories of Dee's wizardry, had broken into his house at Mortlake. Much of Dee's fabulous library was destroyed. This was in 1584, the same year that Laski decided he could no longer afford his expensive guests. Dee, Kelley, and their wives moved to Bohemia as the guests of King Rudolf II. The king was an avid alchemist himself and welcomed the great men.

They divided their time between the palace of Rudolf and that of Count Rosenberg of Trebona, for whom Kelley tried to make an elixir of life to restore the count's lost youth. During this time, Kelley was becoming intolerable. He and Dee quarreled almost constantly, but since Kelley's scrying was Dee's only way to contact the angels, he stayed with the increasingly vicious man.

Finally Kelley irritated Rudolf so badly that the king had him thrown in a dungeon. Apparently Rudolf thought that Kelley had discovered the secret of making the red powder and was holding out on the king. Dee was not bothered—possibly because of his known friendship with Queen Elizabeth. However, Dee left and went to Prague.

Kelley convinced the king that he could make the powder if he could consult with Dee. Rudolf sent Kelley under guard to Prague, but Kelley killed one of the guards while trying to escape. He was then imprisoned in an ancient castle. Dee, alarmed at the turn of events, took his family back to England. This was in 1589. He and Kelley had spent six years in their futile attempt to create gold.

Elizabeth welcomed her favorite magician back to England. She issued an order that he was not to be molested in his magical studies, but she refused to pay for his destroyed library. She did help by appointing him warden of the College of Manchester. This provided Dee a bare living, but brought him into conflict with professors at the college who resented both Dee's fame and his occult leanings.

Back in Bohemia, Kelley made a rope ladder by tying his bed clothes together. He tried to climb out a window of the castle turret where he was imprisoned.

The rope broke and he fell, breaking both legs and sustaining internal injuries. He died soon after.

Dee continued to have misfortunes. He became so feeble that he could no longer handle his duties at the university. He resigned and went back to Mortlake. Queen Elizabeth died and King James I abhorred magic and magicians. The new monarch refused all of Dee's pleas for aid.

The old man barely made a living as a fortune-teller. When this failed, he sold some of the remaining books in his library. About half had been destroyed when he was in Europe, but about two thousand volumes and manuscripts remained. It was said that the old magician wept each time he was forced to sell a book.

He finally died in 1608 and was buried near his home at Mortlake.

Although he associated with an out-and-out rascal, Edward Kelley, Dee's own sincerity was never questioned by the intellectuals of his day. Much of Dee's bad reputation which resulted in attacks on his house and library was due to Kelley's actions. These the superstitious attributed to Dee as well.

One of Kelley's crimes that contributed to Dee's reputation for wizardry was an attempt at necromancy. While a necromancer is a person who practices prophecy through use of the dead, it has come to mean a sorcerer in the public mind. Kelley tried to use the dead in necromancy's first sense. According to an account left by John Weever, a writer of the time:

> He [Kelley] caused a poor man who had been
> buried in the yard belonging to Law Church, near
> to Wotton-in-the-Dale, to be taken out of his
> grave and invoked the spirit of the departed to
> answer to such questions as were put to him.

Sax Rohmer refers to a manuscript in the Bodleian Library which verifies Weever's story and claims Weever got his information from an accomplice of Kelley's who assisted in the forbidden rites in the dark of the night. Some modern books on magic identify Kelley and Dee in an old woodcut showing the necromancers at work. This is not correct. At no time in the original documents was there any suggestion that Dee was present or even knew about it.

While Dee's reputation as a magician is unfortunately confused with Kelley's, there is no question that he was a sincere scientist and held the high regard of his peers. He brought the same sincerity to his work in magic. His downfall as a magician was that, like Faust, he learned all that books could teach him. Where Faust turned to Mephistopheles to bring about his downfall, Dee found his human Mephistopheles in Edward Kelley. This does not deny the point that Dee was a true occult scientist who sincerely believed in magic and worked hard to learn its secrets.

❖ 8 ❖

The Great Charlatan:
Cagliostro

Of all the great magicians, Faust is probably the best known to the general public. Close behind him is Cagliostro. This strange and audacious man was a faker, a charlatan, a rogue, and a scoundrel. He is included here because he is too famous to leave out of a book on magic, and also because at one time in his life he was a sincere student of the art. He believed in magic and earnestly sought its secrets. When he failed, instead of calling on the Devil for assistance as Faust did or turning to a faker (the infamous Edward Kelley) as John Dee did, Cagliostro turned charlatan himself. And we must admit that he did it in the grand tradition.

There are two versions of Cagliostro's early life. One is his own. The other is from investigations made by the

The Count di Cagliostro in a pastel drawing from the Harry Houdini collection

Catholic Church. Most investigators prefer to believe the Church's version.

Cagliostro wrote his account while imprisoned in the Bastille in Paris. He wrote:

> I am ignorant not only of my birthplace, but even of my parents. All my research into my birth and parentage have brought me nothing but vague and uncertain (but in truth exalted) information. My earliest infancy was passed in the town of Medina, in Arabia, where I was reared under the

name of Acharat. This name I used afterwards in my Asiatic and African travels.

I was lodged in the palace of the mufti. I remember having four people with me. One was a tutor. His name was Altotas and he was between fifty-five and sixty years of age. There were three slaves. One was white. The other two were black. My tutor told me that I had been left an orphan when I was three months old, and that my parents were noble, and Christian as well. But he preserved an absolute silence as to their name and to the place where I was born. However, certain things he said caused me to believe I first saw the light in Malta.

Altotas took pleasure in cultivating my natural taste for the sciences. He himself was proficient in them all, from the most profound to the most trivial.

Although his early religious education was Moslem, Cagliostro insisted that "the true religion was engraved on my heart." After growing up, he and Altotas traveled widely in Asia and Africa. When his old tutor died, Cagliostro came to Europe.

The Church's account, plus those of others who have probed into the background of this fascinating rascal, tells a different story. However, they all did find that Cagliostro mixed some fact with his fanciful tale.

These accounts claim that he was born Joseph Balsamo, the son of a small merchant, in Palermo, Sicily, in 1743. Later there were claims that the family was originally Jewish. There is no proof of this, and certainly the family was strongly Catholic at the time young Joseph was born.

The father died when the boy was young, and his widowed mother could not control the wild boy. So his uncle took Joseph into his house—and lived to regret it. He put the boy in a seminary, but Joseph climbed over the wall. He joined a gang of street thieves until his uncle found him. He was then sent to a school run by Benedictine monks. He stayed long enough to learn something about medicine and to allay the suspicions of the good fathers. Then he climbed the wall again.

For the next several years, he lived as best he could, working as a thief and forger. After a couple of sentences to jail, he swindled a goldsmith out of considerable money. With this as capital, he set out to see the world. His first stop was Messina, the seaport in northeast Sicily, where he hoped to find a ship to Egypt. It was here that he met Altotas, the man he called his tutor in his fanciful autobiography.

Altotas was quite a different person from the grave and wise tutor Balsamo pictured. He habitually wore a long gown over European trousers. His head was covered with a silk turban. He always carried an umbrella and led an Albanian greyhound on a leash.

Altotas' strange appearance attracted Balsamo, and he struck up a conversation with the colorful man. Altotas changed the subject each time Balsamo tried to learn something about him, but offered to tell the younger man's fortune. Balsamo then asked if Altotas was a sorcerer. Altotas laughed scornfully, replying that only fools mistook occult science for sorcery. He invited Balsamo to visit him the next day, pointing out the house where he lived.

Balsamo was there at the appointed time. He knocked and the door opened, apparently by itself, for the visitor could see no person near it. Balsamo found himself in a narrow hall, lighted by a candle lamp set in an iron casing on the wall. He followed the corridor and came out in an alchemical laboratory where Altotas greeted him.

Earlier Altotas had warned Balsamo that a thief would try to steal his gold. When Balsamo returned to his quarters he did surprise a thief ransacking the room. This clairvoyance convinced young Balsamo that Altotas was a real magician. The sight of this alchemical laboratory crystallized his belief.

According to Francoise Dumas, a biographer of Cagliostro, the young man had been eagerly studying Hermetic magic for some time. Impressed by Balsamo's knavery, Altotas invited the young man to accompany him to Egypt. The two, living by their wits when Balsamo's money ran out, spent forty days in Alexandria studying Hermetic magic. They supposedly traveled to other parts of Africa, and then to the island of Malta.

Malta was the home of the Order of the Knights of St. John, a secret lodge that traced its history back through the Knights of Rhodes to the Crusaders. The Grand Master of the Order was Manuel Pinto, a Portuguese, who was deeply interested in magic himself. He welcomed Altotas and Balsamo, taking particular

Lorenza (also known as Seraphina) Cagliostro, wife of the great charlatan Joseph Balsamo

interest in the young man. According to Dumas: "Dom Manoël Pinto taught young Balsamo the inner meaning of occultism: the discovery of the transcendent lying behind tangible reality. . . ."

Altotas died while they were in Malta. Then when Pinto died in 1773, Balsamo left Malta to return to Italy. He married a fifteen-year-old girl whom authorities agree was one of the beauties of her time. Casanova, whose reputation as a great lover has survived the years, saw and described her as a "ravishing beauty." In any event, Lorenza joined Balsamo in his wanderings and schemes. By this time, Balsamo had decided that he needed a more august name, and now called himself the Comte de Cagliostro, taking the name from his mother's side of the family.

The two were involved in a number of shady schemes, including blackmail. They left Italy, traveling to France, Spain, and England. Then, in 1774, they went back to France where Lorenza, now calling herself Seraphina, ran off with a Frenchman. Cagliostro had her jailed as an erring wife. After she served her jail sentence, they went back together.

They next appeared in London, where they gave the appearance of having great wealth. Cagliostro's reputation as a magician was increasing. As a result, a man named Scot brought him a strange cabalistic manuscript that was supposed to be a key to gambling success. Scot did not know how to use it and sought Cagliostro's aid. The Sicilian magus studied the manuscript and selected a number as the winner in an upcoming lottery.

Scot was not too impressed, but ventured a small bet on the number. It won. Scot returned to Cagliostro for another number. It also was a winner, as were two later ones. At this point Cagliostro learned that Scot was a swindler instead of the society man he pretended to be. He refused to have any more dealings with Scot. The man became frantic. He was certain that Cagliostro could use cabalistic magic to pick lottery numbers. He used every means from attempted bribery to threats to get Cagliostro to give him more winning numbers. When this failed Scot got a woman accomplice to accuse Cagliostro of stealing a necklace from her. She claimed that he took the gems under pretense of using magic to enlarge them for her. The case came to court and Cagliostro paid a stiff fine. This caused him and Seraphina to leave England.

During his first trip to London, Cagliostro had been fascinated by tales of a strange man who called himself the Comte de Saint-Germain. He is one of the more mysterious figures in the history of magic. No one ever found out who he really was or where he came from. He was very smooth and aristocratic and became a personal friend of Louis XV of France and Frederick the Great of Prussia.

Saint-Germain never personally claimed to be two thousand years old, but, passing a painting of Christ on the cross, he burst into tears, saying, "He was a fine man. I knew him well!"

He also spoke of meeting with the Queen of Sheba. Once when he was talking about an ancient Roman acquaintance, he turned to his servant for confirmation. The servant replied, "I do not know, sir. I have only been in your employ for five hundred years."

Like all good liars, Saint-Germain could prove his lies when backed into a corner. At a royal party he was talking to a duchess. He spoke of meeting her in Italy many years before. She challenged him. Saint-Germain was obviously a man in his forties, and she had not been in Italy in that many years. He could not have known her then. Saint-Germain smiled and related to her certain personal incidents that she swore no one but herself could possibly have known. If this did not prove that Saint-Germain had found a way to keep eternally young, then he had occult means of finding out things.

Saint-Germain became Cagliostro's hero, replacing the dead Altotas. At this point in his life, Cagliostro still believed in magic. He decided that he had reached the point in his studies when he could approach Saint-Germain and convince the great master to take him as a student. So he and Seraphina, leaving London, went to Holstein where Saint-Germain was then in residence.

He had heard of Cagliostro and his beautiful wife. He agreed to meet them, but set two A.M. as the time. Cagliostro and Seraphina came dressed in flowing white robes. They were met by a tall man who spoke no words. He motioned them into a long corridor. A door opened itself before them and they came into Saint-Germain's throne room. The room was lighted by candles and acolytes held braziers from which the smoke of incense rose in the air. The walls were tremendous mirrors. There was a huge altar and Saint-Germain was enthroned upon it. He was dressed in a long robe and had a large diamond pentagram on his chest.

Saint-Germain did not speak, but a voice sounded out of nowhere, asking who the visitors were and why they had come.

Cagliostro and Seraphina prostrated themselves. Then Cagliostro said that he had come to invoke the Father of Truth, to seek of him a secret, and to proclaim himself Saint-Germain's slave and apostle.

The man on the throne said nothing, but the voice

inquired: "And what does the partner of thy wanderings desire?"

Seraphina replied that she wanted only to serve and obey the master of magic.

The candles were snuffed out. An awesome voice from the darkness said, "Woe to those who fail the test!"

Cagliostro and Seraphina were separated to undergo their initiation tests. The tests, while not as elaborate, appear to have been based upon those of the Egyptian mysteries as described by Iamblicus fourteen hundred years earlier (pp. 24-30).

After passing the tests, the two initiates were warned, "The secret of our great art is the government of mankind, and the one means to rule mankind is never to tell mankind the truth."

From this we can infer that Saint-Germain had visions of being a world emperor, although he expressly denied any political motives.

After the initiation rituals, there was a banquet. Then Saint-Germain talked seriously with his new apostles. This talk completely changed Cagliostro's outlook on magic and philosophy in general. Earlier he spoke freely about magic to all who would listen. Saint-Germain taught him to cloak magic in mystery.

Quoting Louis Figuier, Sax Rohmer says:

> His [Cagliostro's] language, his mien, his manner, all are transformed. His conversation turns only upon his travels in Egypt, to Mecca, and to other

remote places, upon the secret sciences into which he was initiated at the foot of the pyramid on the *arcana* of nature which he has discovered. At the same time, he talks little, and more often envelops himself in mysterious silences. When interrogated, he only deigns, for the most part, to draw his symbol—a serpent with an apple in its mouth and pierced by a dart—meaning that human wisdom shall be silent respecting the mysteries it has unravelled.

It would appear from this that Saint-Germain gave Cagliostro the same advice that Trithemius gave Agrippa: there are things about magic best left unsaid.

Cagliostro now became a magic healer. He traveled through the country practicing his art. Unlike other charlatans, he took no money for his work, even preparing the magic medicines at his own expense. We can deduce his motives from a statement made at the time: "He is a good Samaritan, who treats the poor without thought of gain, and sells, for a consideration, immortality to the rich." In other words, Cagliostro's free clinics were an advertisement to build a reputation that could command fabulous prices for the Elixir of Life he secretly sold to the rich.

He and Seraphina went to Russia. Empress Catherine the Great has left a letter claiming Cagliostro was caught faking cures. However, when the court physician rejected the magus' claims, Cagliostro threw down a challenge. He proposed they both swallow poisoned pills.

"Then I will drink my Elixir and be cured. And you cure yourself—if you can!" The doctor refused the challenge.

Cagliostro never recorded the formula for his Elixir, but since he was an earnest student of Edward Kelley, he may have used the Englishman's universal medicine. That elixir was prepared from a base of Hungarian gold and mercury. According to Kelley's account: "Then calcine [that is, change to a powder by heat] it most subtily, with flowers of sulphur and spirit of wine burnt, so often til there remains a subtle gold calx [powder of a purple color]."

Then one takes the "red matter," presumably a material similar to that found in the casket of St. Dunstan, and grinds it and the calx together on a warmed marble for an hour. The mixture is then baked on a fire for three hours. This must be a "circle fire." It is not clear if he means the fire must be in a round shape, or if a circle of fire surrounds the baking material.

The baking is repeated three times and the resulting material is soaked in three fingers of rectified spirit. The mixture is set in a warm place for "gentle digestion." After six days the tincture is poured off. This is sealed in a bottle and set in a "vaporous fire of the first degree. Let it be that the heat is as hot as the sun shines in July. Let it stand for forty days."

The result is the *Aurum Potabile*, a medicine that, taken in an appropriate manner, cures all diseases without pain. But what is the "red matter" and the "appropriate manner?" Like all magical formulae, this was not revealed because of the harm Hermetic magic can cause when practiced by an uninitiate. The rationale for this goes back to the legend of the Sorcerer's Apprentice and all great magicians have observed it. As to whether they knew more or just kept silent to seem more wise is something we must accept on faith—or prove our point through our own experiments.

Cagliostro apparently had been inducted into the secret order on Malta. He continued to travel, investigating freemasonry wherever he went. From Russia, he made several trips to England and then came back to France to establish his own form of freemasonry, according, he claimed, to ancient Egyptian rites. He drew inspiration from Iamblicus and freemasonry, but made great modifications drawn from his own imagination.

He also established a branch for women, over which Seraphina presided. These rites were held in a home separate from the men's, taking their basic form from the ancient Greek women's mysteries. Louis Figuier (in his *Histoire du merveilleux*) gave a description of the initiation rites. The ceremony was limited to exactly thirty-six women, who paid well in gold for the privilege.

The ceremony began just before midnight. The ladies were required to undress and don simple white robes. Each was given a veil to wear. They were conducted into the temple where they found Seraphina seated on a throne. She was guarded by two tall figures enveloped in veils so that nothing about them could be seen.

At Seraphina's command, two young women entered and bound all thirty-six women together with silken ropes. The ropes symbolized women's bondage. She urged them to cast aside the shameful bonds men had placed upon them and cried out for the emancipation of women. Then the ropes were cast aside and the women led into the garden "where they met with most incredible experiences."

They were then taken back into the temple. The light was darkened to that of twilight. A door opened in the roof and a sphere of gold was lowered through it. A naked man stood atop the sphere. It was Cagliostro. He was crowned with a flaming star and held a serpent in his hand.

Seraphina reverently introduced him as the divine and immortal leader, born without a mother from the bosom of Abraham, and the receiver of all knowledge in the universe.

He ordered them to drop their gowns and face the initiation as naked as himself. Then he gave them a lecture on the meaning of the Egyptian rites, which he had brought from the secret heart of the Orient for the happiness of mankind. They had, he said, proven in the garden earlier that they were worthy of receiving instruction in the ancient wisdom that had long been denied to them. This instruction would be given to them by degrees. It would bring them material joy and spiritual peace. Then, at a signal, Cagliostro was raised on his golden sphere back into the roof.

During this time, Cagliostro gave dinner parties at which he promised to raise any dead person of fame whom his guests wished to question. In this respect, he behaved as a carbon copy of Saint-Germain, even repeating the older magus' claim of having personally known Jesus Christ. This he did to the satisfaction of his guests.

All of this was duly reported around, of course, and Cagliostro's fame became overwhelming. Then it all came crashing down and he and Seraphina suddenly found themselves prisoners in the dreaded Bastille prison.

An adventuress named Countess de La Motte told Cardinal de Rohan, a friend of Cagliostro's, that Queen Marie Antoinette wanted to borrow money to buy a magnificent diamond necklace. The cardinal, eager to be appointed a court minister, gave his own note to obtain the necklace for the queen, who did not want the king to know of her extravagance. De Rohan then gave the necklace to a woman he thought was the queen during a meeting at night.

It then came out that the cardinal had been duped. The necklace disappeared and he was stuck with a dun from the jewelers to make good the note he signed. Queen Marie Antoinette heard of the scandal and was enraged. She demanded the arrest of the cardinal and Countess de La Motte. The countess retaliated by trying to throw all the blame on Cagliostro. He and Seraphina were arrested and thrown in the Bastille.

Authorities are at odds over whether Cagliostro was one of the conspirators or whether he was innocent, dragged into the scandal by the vengeful adventuress who was known to hate the magician. The French police were unable to find evidence to connect Cagliostro with the scandal. He and Seraphina were released but ordered out of France. They went to London, where Cagliostro wrote a bitter and spiteful *Letter to the French People*, in which he condemned the royal court that had exiled him without reason. In the letter he predicted the French Revolution.

Cagliostro immediately came under attack by an English journalist and was finally forced to leave the country. Both in France and England men were digging into his past. Claims were made that he was really Joseph Balsamo, but he indignantly denied it.

Leaving London, Cagliostro went to Switzerland and then to Sardinia. He was not welcomed anywhere. Finally, very much against Seraphina's advice, he returned to Rome. Incredibly, he formed an Egyptian rites lodge in the Eternal City, which got him promptly arrested by Vatican authorities. He was tried for sorcery and condemned to death by the church court. On April 7, 1791, the verdict was announced to Pope Pius VI.

His Holiness commuted the sentence to life imprisonment, saying, "Giuseppe Balsamo, accused and convicted of many crimes, and of having defied the censures and penalties pronounced against heretics, dogmatists, masters, and disciples of superstitious magic, as well as the apostolic laws of Clement XII and Benedict XIV against those who in any way whatsoever support and form Societies of Freemasons: now, by special grace, is committed to prison for life in a fortress, where he shall be closely guarded, without hope of grace. . . ."

Cagliostro was imprisoned in Castle San Angelo in Rome. Seraphina was imprisoned in a convent and was never heard of again. The magician himself died in his castle dungeon. One rumor claimed that he strangled himself. There is no proof. Both the time and the manner of his death are unknown. Records are said still to be in the Vatican archives, but no one has ever been permitted to see them. An official life of the magician, based upon the results of the church's inquiry into his life, was published.

We are not concerned here with Cagliostro's offenses against the Church or his involvement in the Affair of the Queen's Necklace, but rather with his work as a magician. There is no question about it: at one time he was a sincere and earnest student of magic. Whether he was a real magician or not is an open question. The person who should have known is Lorenza (Seraphina), the girl he married and who shared his magical wanderings.

She was questioned intensely and harshly by the Church. In one of her statements she said that many of

Cagliostro's effects were prepared in advance, but some were not. The latter, she said, "I assumed were really done by magical art."

This may not be true, but it would appear to be an honest belief on her part. She was confessing to a Church court that would be inclined to be easier on crooks and charlatans than upon persons proclaiming themselves true magicians.

Whatever he was, Cagliostro was a fascinating person. Perhaps more has been written about him than about any other magician who ever lived.

❖ 9 ❖

The Man Who Was Zanoni:
Edward Bulwer-Lytton

Edward Bulwer was born in 1803, the son of a general in the British army. After inheriting his mother's estate, he added her family name to his and became Edward Bulwer-Lytton, the name by which he is known to history.

Bulwer-Lytton is best known as the author of the famous novel *The Last Days of Pompeii,* which is still read today for its graphic descriptions of the burial of Pompeii, a Roman city, by the massive eruption of the volcano Vesuvius in A.D. 79. He was also a well-known politician in his time. Occultists remember him, however, as a serious and profound student of magic.

In the introduction to one of Bulwer-Lytton's books, a writer signing himself W.H. wrote: "One of the peculiarities of Bulwer was his passion for occult science. . . . He became absorbed in wizard lore. He equipped himself with magical implements—with rods for transmitting influence, and crystal balls in which to discern coming scenes . . . and communed with spiritualists and mediums."

This is all true, although statements like "communed with spiritualists and mediums" gives a false impression. The most famous medium of the time was D. D. Home. Home worked hard to get Bulwer-Lytton's endorsement. Home's wife later wrote that it was the one great disappointment of Home's life that he did not get it, though Bulwer-Lytton had Home as a house guest and attended several of the spiritualist's séances.

At the first Home séance Bulwer-Lytton attended, a spirit—speaking through Home's mediumship—told the famous guest, "I am the spirit who inspired you to write *Zanoni.*"

The author's only comment was, "Indeed."

It was made so noncommittally that it might have been a question or an acknowledgment. *Zanoni* was the famous occult novel Bulwer-Lytton wrote.

Bulwer-Lytton was a serious student of the occult, but he rarely discussed it. The one major exception to his silence is his novel *Zanoni,* the plot of which came to the writer in a dream. However, he put into the book the basic magic secrets he had learned in his studies.

Bulwer-Lytton brings this out in his introduction to the novel. He uses the literary device of having the manuscript given to him by a strange old man who belonged to an ancient occult society. Bulwer-Lytton asked if the manuscript was a romance. The answer

Edward Bulwer-Lytton, shown in an engraving as he looked when he wrote *Zanoni*

was: "It is a romance and not a romance. It is truth. It is a truth for those who can comprehend it, and an extravagance for those who cannot."

Students of magic believe this is a true statement. What this means is that the author wrote a book of occult-science fiction. He did exactly what Jules Verne, H. G. Wells, and the legion of science fiction writers who followed them have done. He wrote a fiction story based upon and interwoven with scientific fact. The difference between Verne and Bulwer-Lytton is that the French science fiction writer used orthodox science and the English author used occult science. Verne's science came from the scientists of his day. Bulwer-Lytton's magical science came from his own lifelong studies of things beyond normal perception.

Bulwer-Lytton's association with the paranormal began when he was still a baby. In his autobiography he repeats a story told by his nurse. She was carrying the child in her arms when a man with a "wild air" stopped her. He asked whose child this was. She replied that it was the son of General Bulwer. The strange man then cried that the child would be a greater man than his father, and would be quite remarkable.

His next unusual experience came when he was twenty-one. He had fallen deeply in love with a beautiful young girl. She died and he felt as if life had lost all meaning for him. One evening, in his despair, he went to her grave and remained there all night. Speaking of this later, he said, "What I suffered in one long, solitary night, I will not say. At dawn I turned from the place, as if rebaptized or reborn. . . . The stage of experience and feeling through which my young life had passed contributed largely to render me whatever I have since become."

Some see in this statement the beginning of the writer's lifelong search for the secrets of the world or worlds beyond.

Bulwer-Lytton was an extravagant, spoiled young

man who was supported by his rich mother. However, she angrily cut off his allowance when he married against her wishes. This was a case where Mother really knew best. Bulwer-Lytton and his bride were absolutely unsuited for each other. Their life together was one long fight. They separated, but even then she continued to hound him as he undertook a political career.

When his mother cut off his allowance at the beginning of his marriage, he said that he would support himself and his wife, Rosina, by writing. His first book failed, but the second was successful. From then until his death, Bulwer-Lytton was one of the most popular novelists of his time.

He and Rosina were visiting Italy in 1833, quarreling as usual. During this time, Bulwer-Lytton visited Pompeii, where excavation work had been going on since 1763. Archaeologists were slowly digging the long-buried city from the volcanic ash that had covered it for almost eighteen hundred years. Much work still remained to be done, but enough had been uncovered to show how great the lost city had been.

Bulwer-Lytton wandered through the roofless walls of the rich homes where magnificent wall paintings still retained their vivid colors. He was especially interested in the arena where the gladiators once fought for their lives.

Later he and some friends were discussing the account of Pompeii's destruction left by Pliny the Younger. Pliny wrote that the ash was so thick in the air that it hid the sun, bringing on a premature night. Then when the real night came, it was so dark that no one could see anything. They had to stumble and feel their way along. Someone then remarked that a blind person who knew the city would have an advantage over people with sight in such a situation.

Bulwer-Lytton was struck by this remark. From it came his conception of the blind flower girl who guided the hero to safety in the climax of *The Last Days of Pompeii,* as the city was being covered by the volcano.

The book was published in 1836. It was an immediate success, and is still read today. Despite its florid style, one-dimensional characters, and old-fashioned sentiment, the book is still worth reading for the author's vivid re-creation of the time of Pompeii. Bulwer-Lytton's scholarship was sound.

In 1831, he was elected to Parliament. Then a political pamphlet he wrote enabled the Whig Party to win reelection. This earned him a knighthood and he became Sir Edward Bulwer. At the same time he was offered a high government post. He turned it down, preferring to continue his writing. He quit Parliament in 1841, but was reelected in 1852. Finally, he became Baron Lytton in 1866, thereby fulfilling the prophecy that he would be a greater man than his father, General George Bulwer.

Bulwer-Lytton never ceased to study magic during these years of politics and feverish writing. Since he said, and commentators on his life have agreed, that his book *Zanoni* "was a truth for those who can comprehend it," we must turn to the book itself to search for what Edward Bulwer-Lytton, student of magic, really believed.

Commentators have called it a Rosicrucian novel. They also claim that Bulwer-Lytton was a secret member of the Rosicrucians. He may have been a member and *Zanoni* may be a Rosicrucian book. This depends upon one's definition of Rosicrucian. There have been many groups calling themselves such, but they differ from each other.

The name Rosicrucian first appeared in Europe about 1598, but did not gain wide interest until 1614. At that time German intellectuals were startled to receive an unusual pamphlet entitled "The Fama of the Fraternity of the Meritorious Order of the Rosy Cross." It was addressed to the "learned in general." The author claimed to be a member of an ancient brotherhood that was concerned with the plight of mankind.

The pamphlet pointed out that the Protestant Reformation had cleansed religion and proposed that men of learning join with the brotherhood in likewise cleaning up and directing science toward a moral renewal of mankind. The brotherhood that would assist them in doing this was identified as a group of "children of light" who were versed in Oriental mysteries.

The founder of the Rosy Cross brotherhood was one C.R.C.—later identified as Christian Rosenkreuze. This man died in 1494. The date of his birth was not given.

Rosenkreuze began studying magic when he was five years old. When he was fifteen he had progressed so rapidly that he was invited by a brother magician to accompany him to Jerusalem. The magician died in Cyprus on the way. Rosenkreuze went on alone, but when he arrived in Damascus, Syria, he heard of a secret society of magicians who lived in a lost city in Arabia.

The boy set out in search of this place, called Damcar. It took him a year to find it, but the sixteen-year-old was welcomed by the Arabian magicians. They told him that it had been foretold that he would come to them.

The boy spent three years in Damcar, studying under these learned magicians. Later they sent him to Egypt to study under other masters, who taught him how to invoke elemental spirits.

Hearing that a branch of the ancient brotherhood was in Spain, he went to join them. He found that they had not been satisfied to work for their magical knowledge. They made a pact with Satan in the manner of Faust. Disgusted, Rosenkreuze went back to Germany where he spent the next five years as a hermit. He worked during this time to put all he had learned into one great book of magic.

Then he gathered some people about him who became the founders of the Rosy Cross or Rosicrucian Brotherhood. By and by Christian Rosenkreuze died. A hundred and twenty years passed. The site of the founder's grave was forgotten. It was rediscovered in 1614 when members of the Brotherhood were remodeling an old building that had served their order since its founding. They found Rosenkreuze's body magically preserved. The tomb under the house was lighted with a magic light, and the walls were painted with mystic symbols.

The discovery of their founder's body encouraged the Brotherhood to print the Fama pamphlet, in hopes of bringing together the intellectuals of the world to work for the good of mankind.

The Fama pamphlet did not give an address to which anyone could reply. Applicants were supposed to post letters that members would see on public bulletin boards. Still another pamphlet appeared in 1616, but no one was successful in contacting the society. After a while interest died out.

Through the years there were rumors of Rosicrucian societies in existence. Finally an open one calling itself the Rosicrucian Society of England was organized in 1836. There is no record of any other group publicly claiming to be a Rosicrucian order in England at this time. So if Bulwer-Lytton actually belonged to a Rosicrucian society as had been claimed, it should have been this one.

However, in a letter he wrote in 1870, three years before his death, Bulwer-Lytton said: "There are reasons why I cannot enter into the subject of the Rosicrucian Brotherhood, a Society still existing, but not under any name by which it can be recognized by those outside its pale. Some time ago a sect pretending to style itself 'Rosicrucian' and arrogating full knowledge of the mysteries of the craft, communicated with me. In reply I sent them the cypher sign of the 'Initiate'—not one of them could construe it."

From this we can deduce three things. The true Rosicrucian Society was secret; it did not use any name that would reveal its activity. Therefore, it could not have been the Rosicrucian Society of England. And since Bulwer-Lytton was able to send the "cypher sign of the 'Initiate' " he was definitely a member of *some* society that practiced Rosicrucian magic.

His statement in 1870 that he could not talk about the Rosicrucians is almost a repetition of what he wrote in the introduction to the 1842 edition of *Zanoni:*

"Who but a Rosicrucian could explain the Rosicrucian mysteries! And can you imagine that any members of that sect, the most jealous of all secret societies, would themselves lift the veil of Isis of their wisdom from the world."

This secrecy did not extend to other Rosicrucian societies organized in England and the United States. They welcomed initiates. The two American Rosicrucian groups—which have no connection with each other—are the Rosicrucian Fellowship, founded in 1907, and the Ancient and Mystic Order Rosae Crucis (AMORC), founded in 1925.

Now if we can believe Bulwer-Lytton, both in his fiction and in his letters written near the end of his life, there is a Rosicrucian Society that hides itself behind another name. It is very old and holds occult secrets of great power. Both Bulwer-Lytton and various later occultists—Rudolf Steiner is one—tell us that some of these secrets are hidden in the pages of *Zanoni*.

So let us turn to *Zanoni*. What is it?

Zanoni is the story of two men. One—Mejnour—is extremely old and wise. The other is Zanoni, who is eternally young, although older than any living man. These two are the sole surviving members of an incredibly ancient society whose members have solved the secrets of the occult. It is their duty to teach descendants of the original members, if these heirs ask to be taught.

Mejnour represents cold scientific truth. He is without love and is a creature of the mind. Zanoni represents love and regard for humanity. Mejnour is the older. It was he who taught Zanoni. We are not told how long ago this was, but there are hints that it was long, long ago. Neither of the men is immortal. They can die, but through their occult magic, they have the means of prolonging their lives.

While in Italy, Zanoni falls in love with Viola, a beautiful actress. Mejnour warns him that this could be the end of his occult powers. Zanoni does not care. He is a creature of love and he needs the love of Viola. It means more to him than extending his loveless life through generation after generation.

But somehow there is something missing in his association with his beloved. Zanoni summons the last of his failing occult powers and conjures up Aidon-Ai, an occult creature of light who has helped Zanoni in generations past.

Curiously, Bulwer-Lytton chose a name for this supernatural entity very similar to the Hebrew word Adon-Ai, which means Lord and is one of the various names of God. He may have intended some obscure symbolism in doing this.

In the exchange between Aidon-Ai and Zanoni, we get a hint that Zanoni was originally from Chaldea, a country that flourished about 5,000 years ago.

Zanoni asks Aidon-Ai if there is no link that can bind his and Viola's souls as their hearts are united.

"Know thou not that when two souls are divided a third in which both meet and live is the link between them?"

Zanoni is overjoyed when a child is born to him and Viola. Then mother and child are stricken with a terrible fever. His own mystic powers diluted by earthly love, Zanoni is unable to call Aidon-Ai to his aid. However, a dreaded woman who is the opposite of the godlike Aidon-Ai and who represents evil does come. This creature, called the Dweller of the Threshold, comes unbidden to taunt the "young Chaldean."

"Young in thy countless ages," the horror cries. "Young as when, cold to pleasure and to beauty, thou stood on the old Fire-tower, and heard the starry silence whisper to thee the last mystery that baffles Death."

She asks if he fears Death at length. "Generation after generation have withered since we two met. Lo! Behold me now!"

Zanoni replies that he beholds her without fear. Although thousands have perished because of her, she is not his vanquisher, "but my slave!"

She replies that she is ready to continue to serve as his slave. "Death is in thy palace! Aidon-Ai comes not to thy call. Only where no cloud of the passion and the flesh veils the eye of the Serene Intelligence can the Sons of the Starbeam glide to man. But *I* can aid thee . . . I can gift thee with the art to save her. I can place healing in thy hand."

Zanoni pauses only to bargain for the child's life as well as the mother's. The Dweller of the Threshold agrees and Zanoni cries, "I yield! Mother and child—save both!"

In this passage it is clear that the Dweller is Death itself and that, in Chaldea five thousand years before, Zanoni learned the secret of opposing Death. He did this through the aid of Aidon-Ai, who is a Christlike figure.

There are definite touches of Hinduism and Buddhism in this exchange between Zanoni and Death. Hinduism, from which Buddhism grew as a reformation, believes that original human souls were sparks thrown out from Brahman, the creator spirit of all creation. It is the duty of these human souls to return to their creator. But since Brahman is perfect, the souls—which have become soiled by the passions of the earth—must be purified before they can return. This is too difficult to do in any one lifetime and Hinduism teaches that reincarnation is necessary for the soul to purify itself over many lifetimes.

In a like manner, the magi of the society to which Mejnour and Zanoni belong must be pure of all earthly passions and desires—complete ascetics—before they can draw upon the powers of the Sons of the Starbeam for their magic. This magic permits them to control the invisible elemental spirits and to hold Death itself at bay. Zanoni lost this power when he fell in love with Viola. A true magician must be without feeling for anything but knowledge. The original Buddha—in contrast to later sects—taught something of the same idea. A person who is seeking Nirvana, the ultimate reunion with Creation, must purge his mind and soul of all worldly passions, hungers, and desires.

We are not told what Zanoni gave up when he told the Dweller "I yield!" We can presume that he has agreed to stop fighting her and will go to his own death.

In any event, the book moves on to its tragic climax. In the French Revolution, Viola and her child are imprisoned. Zanoni is beheaded in the Reign of Terror. When he goes to the guillotine, Viola in her cell receives a lightning flash of inspired knowledge. "The true meaning of his mystic gift, the very sacrifice he made for her, all became distinct for a moment to her mind. . . ."

The Reign of Terror ends that night with the death of Robespierre, the butcher who brought it on. People opening the prison cells to let out the prisoners "burst into a cell, forgotten since the previous morning. They found there a young female . . . never had they seen life so beautiful . . . but as they crept nearer . . . they saw that the beauty and ecstasy were of death. . . . At her feet was a young infant, who looked at them steadfastly, and with its rosy fingers played with its dead mother's robe."

A woman with the rescue group says, "Alone in the world, what can be its fate?"

A priest with them replies, "The orphan smiles! The Fatherless are the care of God!"

Running through the novel is a subplot dealing with an artist, Glyndon, whose ancestor was a member of the Brotherhood. Zanoni agrees to teach him to be one of them, but Mejnour takes over this duty when Zanoni's powers fade. It is in this teaching that we must look for the occult science that Bulwer-Lytton wove into his book. Whether or not this is true occult science or a delusion is something each investigator must decide individually.

One point Bulwer-Lytton does make—speaking through Mejnour—is that the ancient society, going back to Chaldea, is Rosicrucian in nature, but it is not one of the groups calling themselves Rosicrucian.

Earlier, Zanoni had told Glyndon: "Do you imagine there was no foundation for those traditions which come dimly down from remoter ages . . . ? What was the old Colchian magic, but the minute study of Nature in her lowliest works? . . . The most gifted of all the Priestcraft, the mysterious sisterhoods of Cuth . . . sought in the meanest herbs what, perhaps, the Babylonian Sages explored in vain amidst the loftiest stars."

Since they were discussing Zanoni's habit of picking

herbs, we infer from this that magic elixirs, compounded from strange plants, played a part in contacting the invisible world and in conquering death.

Rosicrucianism also creeps in in Book II Chapter VI, when Glyndon wonders: "Did Zanoni belong to this mystical Fraternity, who, in an earlier age, boasted of secrets of which the Philosopher's Stone [which could turn base metal to gold] was but the least; who considered themselves the heirs of all that the Chaldeans, the Magi, the Gymnosophists, and the Platonists had taught; and who differed from all the darker sons of Magic in the virtue of their lives, the purity of their doctrines, and their insisting, as the foundation of wisdom, on the subjugation of the senses . . . a glorious sect if it lied not!"

Zanoni echoes this when he tells Glyndon later: "No neophyte must have, at his initiation, one affection or desire that chains him to the world. He must be pure from the love of woman, free from avarice and ambition, free from the dreams even of art, or the hope of earthly fame."

In Book IV, called "The Dweller on the Threshold," Mejnour reveals something of the true Rosicrucian Brotherhood. After the young man asks if Mejnour and Zanoni "profess to be brothers of the Rosy Cross," he tells Glyndon:

"Do you imagine that there were no mystic and solemn unions of men seeking the same end through the same means before the Arabians of Damus [Damcar] taught to a wandering German [Christian Rosenkreuze] the secrets that founded the Institution of the Rosicrucians? I allow, however, that the Rosicrucians form a sect descended from the greater and earlier school."

Glyndon asks who survives of this earlier school. Mejnour replies: "Zanoni and myself."

In speaking of their ability to live for over five thousand years, Mejnour denies that they have immortality. He says that a wall might at that moment fall and crush him. "All we profess to do," he said, "is to find out the secrets of the human frame; to know why the parts harden and the blood stagnates. Then we apply continual preventives to the effects of time. This is not magic. It is the art of medicine rightly understood."

Going deeper into metaphysics, Mejnour points out that astronomy has shown man that his world is just a speck in space. The microscope has revealed minute life that proves that a drop of water holds more living things by number than the entire world of men.

"Is it not a visible absurdity to suppose that beings are crowded upon every leaf, and yet absent from the immensities of space? . . . How can you conceive that space, which is the Infinite itself, is alone lifeless. . . . No microscope is yet invented to discover the nobler things that hover in the air. Yet between these last and man is a mysterious and terrible affinity. And thence by tales and legends, not wholly false nor wholly true, have arisen from time to time, beliefs in apparitions and spectres."

As a test of Glyndon's qualities to be a magician,

A drawing from an 1897 edition of *Zanoni* shows Mejnour conjuring up the invisible creatures of air and space for his student Glyndon.

Mejnour leaves him in the castle alone, with strict orders not to pry into the laboratory secrets. Glyndon
disobeys and is almost killed by elements he conjures
up. Mejnour then rejects him as a student.

In a note appended to the second edition of *Zanoni,*
(1853) a person identified only as "an eminent writer,"
says: "The curiosity which *Zanoni* has excited among
those who think it worthwhile to dive into the subtler
meanings they believe it intends to convey, may excuse
me in adding a few words, not in explanation of its
mysteries, but upon the principles which permit them.
Zanoni is not, as some have supposed, an allegory. But
beneath the narrative it relates, *typical* meanings are
concealed."

There you have it. For more than 130 years, men
have been saying that there are occult secrets hidden in
Zanoni. This is not to say these claims are right or
wrong. Regardless of the truth or untruth, it is interest-
ing to contemplate. As Mejnour told Glyndon: "Who is
there in youth that has not nourished the belief that the
universe has secrets not known to the common herd,
and panted for the fountains that lie hid and far away
amidst the broad wilderness of trackless science? . . .
Think you that none who have cherished the hope have
found the truth? . . . No!"

Zanoni has survived the years and copies can still be
found in some of the larger libraries. So anyone who
feels that it does contain occult truth is free to puzzle
over its pages.

However, what it has to say is not intelligible unless

one already knows a great deal about the occult. So this puts the seeker after knowledge in the same position as the young person seeking a first job. The employer will not take anyone without experience, but how does one get experience if none will employ him? This may be why so many would-be magicians, frustrated in their search, turned to devil worship as the easier way.

The Cabalist—
Eliphas Lévi

Magic has always been with us. At different times in history magic has gone underground to escape official and public censure. However, devotees have always kept it alive in secret orders and cults. Then, when the conditions were right, it surfaced again and historians say it had a "revival."

The man who called himself Eliphas Lévi is credited with having "revived" magic in France. This is hardly correct. Since the scandalous days of Cagliostro and the mad Comte de Saint-Germain magic had fallen into public disrepute, but it was a long way from dead. What Lévi did was to bring magic back into the open and make it publicly popular again.

The name Lévi suggests a Jewish cabalist, but Lévi was really Alphonse Louis Constant, a Catholic who fulfilled all the requirements for the priesthood and then refused ordination at the last minute. He became one of the giants of nineteenth-century magic.

Bridging Cagliostro and Lévi were such men as Martines de Pasqually and Pierre Michael Eugene Vintras, along with Mesmer the hypnotist and others. Pasqually was a mysterious wanderer in the tradition of Saint-Germain. He founded a freemasonry order with ceremonial magic based partly on the Catholic Mass and partly on Cornelius Agrippa. Vintras operated a secret society that had considerable trouble because of its association with a pretender to the French throne. Mesmer was not a true magician in the classic sense of the word. He was a healer through the use of "animal magnetism," which became hypnotism.

The magician who would outstrip them all in fame was born in Paris in 1810, and was baptized Alphonse Louis Constant. He was a dreamy, withdrawn child who spent much time alone. When he was ten the boy was accepted in a school that local priests ran for the sons of poor families. While there he developed an almost supernatural attitude toward the Catholic religion, and the priests picked him as a likely candidate for the priesthood.

At the same time he came under the influence of a priest-teacher with religious-occult interests. In later life Constant said that this man—Abbé Frère—opened vast views of progress and the future for him. Even so, the father's narrow view of religion and obsolete ideas caused his young student "to walk for some time along a false path." Later, when the priest was dismissed because of his views, Constant became disillusioned with his religion.

This disillusionment grew when he attended the theological college at Saint-Sulpice. He found the place, the students, and the instructors cold and—in his view—suspicious, as well as narrow-minded. He studied hard, however, passed the first three orders, and was ordained a subdeacon. Only one step remained until his ordination as a full-fledged priest.

As a result of his great piety, he was selected to teach catechism classes to the young daughters of the best families in the town. He loved it, and the children in turn loved this young man who was not above dropping his reverent remoteness and laughing with them. He said later that the children made him feel like a father surrounded by his children.

During this time a very poor woman brought her own daughter to the young student. She had no money to pay for lessons and asked him to teach the girl out of charity.

Constant readily agreed, but found the girl—who was older than the children he had been teaching—disturbing to him. This caused him to doubt his ability to continue in the priesthood. He claimed later that he was not in love with the girl. "But through her I had felt awakened in me the need to love." We can doubt his protests, for it seems that he was indeed in love with the girl, Adèle Allenbach.

In any event, he underwent a long, agonizing struggle with his conscience and his beliefs. He found that his interest in magic had caused him unconsciously to wander away from Church teaching. Now his human feeling, together with his magical leanings, made him decide that he could not go on within the confines of organized religion. He refused ordination into the priesthood, leaving the seminary to embark on a course that would make him the most influential magician of his time. Part of his enormous influence was due to his refusal to fight religion. He never left his basic Catholicism, but tried to justify religion in terms of cabalistic magic. This, of course, brought him high censure from some quarters.

He was then twenty-six. His father had died and his mother killed herself. Now in a world for which his lifelong religious life had not prepared him, he was miserable and the future appeared bleak. He supported himself by teaching in a small school for a year. Then a childhood friend offered to take him into an acting troupe that toured the French provinces. From all reports, Constant made a good actor.

The important thing in his life that resulted from his short acting career was that he met Flora Tristan. Mme Tristan was the grandmother of the famous French painter Paul Gauguin. She was a very beautiful woman, but was considered scandalous. She had divorced her husband at a time when nice women did not do such things. Then she became one of the first labor union agitators. She wrote books on socialism and was considered an anarchist. Mme Tristan was amused by

Constant's unworldliness and introduced him around in socialist and literary circles. This had a great influence in developing the young man's own literary career.

Association with Mme Tristan and her friends led Constant into trouble. He absorbed some of their socialistic beliefs and wrote a book that landed him and the publisher in jail. More trouble came when he began a romance with the headmistress of a school and then hastily married one of her teenage students. Mme Constant became a writer herself and the marriage was quite happy for several years. Then she ran off with her publisher.

During these years he continued his study of magic and began writing on the subject, coming under the influence of Hoene Wronski. Wronski was a Polish fugitive who was working on magical mathematics, which he hoped would explain the universe. But despite various occult influences, the most important influence on Constant was the Jewish Cabala. Constant had never forgotten his basic Catholic training, and the Cabala, which is supposed to be the secret wisdom hidden in the Bible, appealed to him, for it seemed to be a fusing of religion and magic. This interest caused him to adopt the Jewish name Eliphas Lévi for his book *Dogme de la magie,* his first major writing on the subject. He kept this name for the rest of his life.

In his unhappiness over his wife's desertion, Lévi went to England. He was welcomed by British occultists and met the famous Bulwer-Lytton, with whom he had long talks about magic. The acquaintance with the author of *Zanoni* led Lévi into a curious adventure.

One day he received a note with a torn card enclosed. The card was marked with the seal of Solomon. The note asked Lévi to be in front of Westminster Abbey the following afternoon. Lévi kept the appointment. He was met by a veiled woman in a carriage. She had the other half of the card to prove that she had sent the message to him.

She was an elderly woman. A friend of Bulwer-Lytton's had suggested that she contact Lévi. She said that Lévi was probably without magical equipment, since such would be awkward to bring from France. She offered Lévi the use of her equipment, provided he pledge himself to secrecy. He promised never to divulge her name or where she lived.

They talked as they drove to her home. Lévi recognized her as a magic adept, but not one of the first order. She believed that magic could not be learned entirely from books. There had to be practical experiments. She was not advanced enough to do this herself, and offered Lévi the use of her rare and expensive equipment if he would evoke the spirit of Apollonius of Tyana.

Lévi inspected her magic cabinet and her vestments, and agreed to conduct the spirit evocation. This required twenty-one days of preparation. She loaned him some ancient books he needed for the rituals.

The cabinet for the evocation was in the form of a turret. There were four mirrors inside and an altar surrounded by a chain of iron that had been magnetized. The top of the altar was marble and the sign of the pentagram was carved on its surface. There was a white lambskin, also marked with the pentagram, under the altar. A small copper chafing dish containing charcoal made from alder and laurel wood lay on the table.

Another chafing dish, mounted on a thin tripod, was placed in front of the magician. Lévi wore a long white gown and was crowned with some leaves entwined with a golden chain. He kindled fires in each of the chafing dishes. Then, taking a new sword in one hand and the book of rituals in the other, he began reading the mystic words. Soon it seemed to him that the earth shook. The white smoke from the fires thickened and seemed to waver. He placed more fuel on the fires, which blazed up anew.

Then, through the leaping flames, Lévi thought he saw the figure of a man. It wavered and disappeared. He put fresh fuel on the fires and recommenced the evocation ritual. A faint form appeared on the cabinet mirror. Lévi closed his eyes and repeated the evocation ritual three times more. When he opened his eyes, he saw a man dressed in a gray shroud. The man was beardless and very thin. He appeared melancholy. He did not look at all as Lévi had expected the great Apollonius of Tyana to look.

The image faded away. Lévi repeated his evocation. Instead, he felt something touch his sword arm. The arm went numb. Lévi deduced that this meant that the sword bothered the spirit. Lévi dropped the point of the sword, which he previously had leveled at the spirit. The spirit reappeared as soon as the point of the sword touched the magic circle in which Lévi stood for protection.

The reappearance of the evoked spirit caused Lévi to feel suddenly weak and he had to sit down. He felt as if he were going to faint. He was supposed to ask Apollonius two questions, one for himself and one for the woman who had asked him to make the evocation. He was unable to speak, but the questions were formed in his mind, and it seemed to him, although the apparition was wordless, that the answers to his questions appeared in his own brain.

The woman wanted information about some man. The answer was: "Death." Lévi wanted to know if he and his lost wife would be reconciled. The answer was: "No."

Lévi then fell into a dreamlike state. He knew that the dreams were strange indeed, but upon regaining his senses he was unable to remember anything about them. His arm, benumbed by the spirit, took several days to regain its total feeling.

In telling of this experience, Lévi asked, "Did I really evoke the great Apollonius of Tyana? I do not believe it. I do not explain the physical laws by which I saw and touched. I affirm solely that I did see and that I did touch. I saw clearly and distinctly."

In telling about this in *Dogme de la magie,* Lévi cautioned his reader about trying the same experiment. It was dangerous, as all evocations of spirits are. It was also, he said, very fatiguing, the fatigue lasting for several days.

Lévi was an adequate, although not a brilliant artist. And when times were bad he supported himself by drawing. One of his commissions was to illustrate Alexandre Dumas' *The Count of Monte Cristo,* a famous novel that is still read today. Dumas liked Lévi's work well enough to take him on as a staff artist for *The Musketeer,* a magazine the writer published for a while. Dumas was the most famous popular writer of his day and was known everywhere. He was fascinated by magic and had written two books about Cagliostro. He introduced Lévi into social circles previously closed to the magician. As a result of this and his growing number of books on magic, Lévi was able to support himself as an occultist.

When he was fifty-four, Lévi moved to a three-room apartment where he was to live the rest of his life. It was definitely a magician's home, overflowing with magical apparatus, old books, and pictures of arcane subjects. Here he received those who came to see him. Some were lunatics. One tried to murder him, another wanted to give him the secret of immortal youth—a secret that was suspect because the giver was old and feeble himself. Some who came were students or rich people seeking magical help or a peek at the future.

The wife of the British consul in Paris left a description of the magician at this time. The woman was taking magic lessons from Lévi. She said he gave the impression of profound peace, but was lively and al-

Eliphas Lévi, the best-known magician of his time, in front of one of his drawings, *The Goat of the Sabbat*

ways in a good humor. He had a brilliant Rabelaisian wit, which carried a hidden meaning. She said that the ignorant could see Lévi's humor simply as amusing jokes, but the initiated could detect the deeper philosophical meaning behind them. In this manner, Lévi was in the tradition of the great magicians who concealed the ultimate truths of their writings. She said that he worked hard to teach magic to those who came to him as students, but he never deceived them as to their ability or how much they could expect from his teaching. Even though he had rejected the priesthood, she said that he was still deeply attached to the Catholic religion.

This attachment to religion, while teaching things condemned by the Church, is a contradiction in Lévi's character that has confused many people who have tried to figure out what the master really believed. The cause of this confusion is that Lévi's religion was basically cabalistic. That is, he believed in the Cabala, which professed to reveal the hidden truths of the Bible. These truths were hidden for the same reason that Trithemius warned Agrippa to avoid saying too much in his books. The full knowledge of the nature of the universe—the true source of what we in our ignorance call magic—is too dangerous for general dispensation. It can be revealed only to the highest rank of initiate who knows how to protect him or herself from tremendous and little-understood forces.

To Lévi, religion is based upon faith. Faith is the seeking of the unknown. Therefore, the basic element of faith is mystery. In one of his books he claimed: "The formula of a mystery must necessarily exclude the secret of that formula. If one understands the formula, then it expresses the known rather than the unknown. It would then belong to science and not to religion, which is faith."

This does not make sense. The true goal of an occult scientist should be to penetrate the unknown and make it known. He should try to turn blind faith, superstition, and ignorance into a demonstrable science. But Lévi loved the mystery of the unknown. He loved ceremonies and rituals—a love that went back to his childhood admiration for the Catholic Mass. He wanted to know enough, but not too much. He wanted to keep mystery and faith.

In one book he said that he was aware that Christianity tries to suppress ceremonial magic. The Tribe of Levi—the priests of the Hebrews of the Exodus—considered the exercise of magic as the usurpation of the priesthood. Lévi claimed that other religions fought magic for the same reason. Magic, in Lévi's view, revealed the truth behind the facade of religion. This was a truth that he also wanted to keep partly hidden, in order to preserve its occult mystery.

A. E. Waite, a prolific writer on magic, summed up Lévi's beliefs. He said that Lévi believed that magic was real, and that it could give man superhuman powers through traditional secrets transmitted from ancient magi.

"Arising from this occult science Lévi believed in," Waite said, "there is one infallible and truly catholic religion that has always existed, but which is unadaptable to the multitude. For this reason, there has come into being the exoteric [something that can be understood by all] religion of fable and nurse's tales. This is all that is possible for the profane. It has undergone many transformations, and is represented at this day [1875] by Latin Christianity under the obedience of Rome."

He goes on to say that this "Latin Christianity" may be called true for the masses, but that "it is magic alone which imparts true science."

All Lévi has done here is to add the "Latin Christianity" to the basic ideas of the Cabala. The whole idea that the rest of us are not learned enough to understand true religion and must be fed parables and fables does not necessarily mean that we are stupid. It means simply that we do not have the knowledge and understanding to comprehend these esoteric secrets, and must depend upon an exoteric explanation that has been simplified for us.

As an example, an Eskimo folktale tells the story of a mighty warrior who was trapped in a giant igloo by forces of evil. He pushed down the key block of ice in the room, causing the walls to fall in and crush the enemy. This sounds like an Eskimo Samson—and this is exactly what he was. Quite a number of years ago, a medical missionary ministering to a backward tribe told them biblical stories, which he translated into their tongue. In the story of Samson, he could not tell them how the biblical strongman pushed down the pillars of stone, because they had never seen pillars and had no concept of them. So he recast the story in terms of a giant igloo and this far northern Samson who pushed down blocks of ice.

"It is by the Cabala, and this alone, that all is explained," Lévi wrote in his introduction to *The History of Magic*. He claimed that the Cabala destroyed nothing in other religions, "but, on the contrary, gives reason to all that is."

In preaching in this manner, Lévi was putting forth nothing new, but he succeeded in convincing a lot of people. This is mainly because Lévi brought into the open what many magicians had been keeping in the dark—that there is no conflict between magic and religion. The two are the same, except that one—magic—goes deeper than the other. There is no such thing as real black magic. There is only magic, although it can be used for either good or evil.

Organized religion, of course, angrily denied such views. And even those who admire Lévi the most must admit that the magician was often confusing and contradictory in what he wrote. It is frequently difficult to grasp exactly what he is driving at, and his books are hard to read. Also, his writings betray the fact that Lévi was not as deep a scholar of magic as he claimed to be. He made many errors, as A. E. Waite points out in his numerous footnotes to the translations he made of Lévi's books.

As far as Lévi the prophet is concerned, in a few years we will have an opportunity to check on his accuracy. He claimed that the earth is ruled over by beings, under direction of God, whom he called

Mitatron-Sarpanim. The first of these was Enoch, the father of Methuselah. After Enoch came Elias (Elijah), and then Jesus Christ. Each of these has two reigns upon the earth. One reign has been completed. The other is to come. Enoch will return in "the year 2000 of the Christian world, then the Messianism of which he will be the forerunner will flourish on the earth for a thousand years." Enoch will be followed by Elijah, who will prepare the earth for the second coming of Christ.

Lévi's last years were spent in pain, but not in poverty. His followers maintained his home and provided doctors for him. He suffered from dropsy and decreased blood circulation that led to gangrene in his limbs. He knew he was dying and took the end calmly. According to one visitor, he had a statue of Christ at the end of his bed where he could look directly in His face. On May 31, 1875, his nurse went to get a priest. Shortly after the priest left, Eliphas Lévi died.

A few months after his death, a child was born in England who would also become a magician. Later, this child would claim to be a reincarnation of Lévi. This hardly seems likely, for Lévi was a kindly man who earnestly sought to help his fellow people and believed that magic and religion were the same. This new magician was as wicked as Lévi was good. Long before his death he was being called "the wickedest man in the world." His name was Aleister Crowley, sometimes known as Beast 666.

❖ 11 ❖

The Wickedest Man in the World: *Aleister Crowley*

I n the Revelation of St. John the Divine there is
an account of a blasphemous beast who had the
horns of a lamb and the voice of a dragon. This
beast came out of the earth, "and he doeth great wonders, so that he maketh fire come down from heaven on
earth in the sight of men."

This beast deceived men by means of miracles. He
had them stained with the mark of the beast either on
their right hand or on their forehead.

"And that no man might buy or sell, save he that had
the mark, or the name of the beast, or the number of
his name.

"Here is wisdom. Let him that hath understanding
count the number of the beast; for it is the number of a
man; and his number is six hundred threescore and
six."

The mother of Aleister Crowley was a deeply religious woman. She was so horrified by the blasphemy and irreligious activity of her son that she angrily called him "the Beast 666," after the beast who came out of the earth as related by John in Revelation 13 and 14.

Crowley was not offended. He gloried in the title and used it in reference to himself for the rest of his life. While he did not have horns on his head and make fire rain from heaven, he did fulfill the prophecy of Revelation by deceiving men by means of what he called miracles, and tried to put the mark of the beast on all who would listen to him. Outraged journalists called him "the wickedest man in the world." He loved the title, as he had his mother's claim that he was the Beast 666, and did his best to live up to it. More than any other man of whom we have clear historical knowledge, Crowley is what the average person thinks of as the wicked magician of legend.

Aleister Crowley was born in 1875 and died in 1947. His father owned a brewery and there was money for private tutors. Later he went to Trinity College, Cambridge, where in 1546 John Dee had been one of the original Fellows. Crowley was above average in intelligence, but showed little interest in studying for a diplomatic career, which was what he was sent to college for. He loved poetry, chemistry, mathematics, chess, and mountain climbing. At the same time he hated religion, ranting often against the puritanism of his mother and his family in general.

While still in college, Crowley privately printed two

books of poetry. While many critics deplored his subject matter, the general opinion was that he was a poet of considerable power.

He did not show much interest in any kind of work except writing. He produced thirty books of various kinds in the next ten years. Almost all of these were printed by himself, or subsidized by him. His family, while deploring his life-style, remained generous in the matter of allowances to him. For a while it seemed that he intended a career as a globe trotter and a mountain climber. In 1900–1902 he made a round-the-world tour.

During this tour, he organized a six-month expedition to climb K-2 in the Himalayas. The climb took sixty-five days on the glacial parts of the mountain alone. The party never reached the top, but turned back at 22,000 feet.

While in Ceylon, a major Buddhist center, he studied Yoga as part of his intense study of magic. This interest started in his childhood and crystallized during his early college years when he read Eliphas Lévi's writing. In India his studies of tantric Buddhism (which weaves sex into its rites) convinced him that reincarnation is true. He convinced himself that he was the reincarnation of Lévi. He justified this claim by saying that he had the same ideas about magic as Lévi even before he was introduced to the French magician's writing. Also, he and Lévi were tied together by death and birth. Lévi died shortly before Crowley was born.

Tibetan Buddhism teaches that when its spiritual leader, the Dalai Lama, dies, his soul immediately flies into the body of a child just being born. Crowley insisted that this was what happened to him. His soul, leaving the dying shell known as Eliphas Lévi, took possession of the about-to-be-born shell that became Aleister Crowley.

In 1898 he joined the famous magical circle known as the Golden Dawn, founded by William Wynn Westcott, W. R. Woodman, and S. L. MacGregor Mathers. Mathers expanded the society and then later took it over entirely. The first lodge of the Golden Dawn was the "Isis-Urania Temple of the Hermetic Order of the Golden Dawn," established in London in 1888. The Golden Dawn was based upon freemasonry, Rosicrucianism, occult Hermetic magic, and the ideas of Mathers.

Many famous people were drawn to the Golden Dawn. Some kept their connection a secret, like Sax Rohmer, author of the Fu Manchu novels, whose connection was not revealed until long after his death. Others, like the famous Irish poet William Butler Yeats, made no secret of their interest in magic and the Golden Dawn. In a letter to a friend, Yeats wrote: "If I had not made magic my constant study I could never have written a single word of my Blake book. . . . The mystical life is the center of all that I do and all that I think and all that I write. . . . I have always considered myself a voice of what I believe to be a greater renaissance—the revolt of the soul against the intellect—now beginning in the world."

Yeats met MacGregor Mathers at an artist's studio in

London. After talking about the occult for some time, Mathers invited the poet to join the Golden Dawn. According to Yeats, Mathers told him, "We only give you the symbols [of magic], because we respect your liberty." By this Mathers meant that he would provide Yeats with the tools to become a magician, but what Yeats did with the tools (rituals and knowledge) was up to the young man.

In his autobiography, written late in his life, Yeats said, "I accepted his invitation to join an order of Christian Kabalists. I am still a member and, though I attend but little, value a ritual full of the symbolism of the Middle Ages and the Renaissance, with many later additions."

Yeats was serious about magic. He believed in it sincerely, and tried to work with those who were equally sincere. Crowley also was serious. At least at this point in his life he believed in it, but—unlike Yeats—he could not work with others unless he dominated them. As soon as Crowley was familiar with the Golden Dawn rituals, he began working to undermine Mathers' authority. The excuse he gave was that Mathers was not doing enough to contact the astral being who could give them the occult wisdom they sought. In actuality, Crowley wanted to take over the order so he could introduce elements of tantric sex worship. Mathers expelled Crowley from the Golden Dawn and later was expelled himself. When Mathers died, Crowley's supporters—with no objection from the Beast 666—put out the story that Mathers died because he was the loser in a duel of magic between himself and Aleister Crowley.

Crowley married Rose Kelly, the sister of Sir Gerald Kelly, a famous painter of the day, and took her with him on his world travels in search of new ideas in magic. These travels were extensive. In this respect, Crowley probably had a wider knowledge of world magic than any person up to his time, since he went everywhere there was magic and studied with local practitioners.

While Crowley and Rose were in Cairo in 1904, she began to have astral stirrings. She was not the psychic type and Crowley at first refused to believe what she told him. This was that a message of transcendant importance was going to be communicated to him to pass on to the world.

Shortly after this an astral being named Aiwass dictated a strange book to Crowley. It was a short message, given to Crowley over a period of three days. It was called *The Book of the Law* and expounded the Law of Thelema, which is: "Do what thou wilt shall be the Whole of the Law."

Crowley identified Aiwass as Shaitan, the devil of ancient Sumer, a civilization of the Tigris and Euphrates delta that is older than Babylon. Shaitan is the root word for Satan, the devil of Christian religions. He was also, according to Crowley, the God who made mankind.

Crowley did not immediately publish *The Book of the Law.* He continued his avid study of magic, which he now spelled magick, adding the *k* to distinguish it from stage conjuring and to establish his brand of magic as different from others.

He became estranged from his wife and formed a homosexual relationship with a poet. The two traveled widely, trying to hone their occult sensitivities with trances and drugs. In one case, they climbed a mountain, drew pentagrams and occult symbols in the dirt, and conducted their magical rituals according to an ancient document Crowley had found. The experiment ended in wild elation gripping the two men, climaxing in activities said to be unnatural even for a man like Crowley.

In the meantime, Crowley had formed his own order and established a magical publication he called the *Equinox*. Despite court action by Mathers to stop him, Crowley exposed the rituals of the Golden Dawn in his publication. By this time the Golden Dawn had split into several factions, none of which could agree with the others. Some of these are still in existence. Several are said to be in Southern California.

It was 1910 before Crowley finally got around to carrying out Aiwass' instruction to carry the Law of Thelema to the world. This began with a public exhibition of a poetical ritual Crowley called *An Invocation to Luna.*

A reporter for the London *Sketch* attended the exhibition, and described it in the August 24, 1910, issue of the paper, under the heading, "A New Religion."

The reporter, who signed his piece with the initials R. R., said the exhibition was held in a room at the

Equinox offices. The room was dark, except for a dull-red light that was directed at an altar. Young men, dressed in robes of either white, black, or red, stood about the room. Several of them held drawn swords. Spectators stood at the back of the room.

Different members of the brotherhood came forward to perform various "magickal" rites to "banish the Pentagram and to purify the temple." Crowley then came forward and led the brotherhood in a "Mystic Circumambulation" of the altar, which consisted of a slow, stately march three times around it. He then called for the Cup of Libation. A brother came forward with a large golden bowl filled with a liquor. The drink was also offered to the spectators. The writer R. R. did not say what it tasted like, but did say that it was pleasant smelling.

The rituals continued. One brother read the "Twelve-told Certitude of God." Then another used a hexagram to call the spirit of the Greek goddess Artemis. Crowley then read a poem, which was followed by another libation from the golden bowl. At this point Crowley brought in a woman draped and hooded in blue, a color R. R. claimed was associated with Hecate, the goddess of witches. He enthroned her behind the altar and then recited a poem by Swinburne.

R. R. claims that "the ceremony had grown weird and impressive." The golden bowl was passed around again and ceremony followed ceremony, climaxing in a "Dance of Pan and the Syrinx [panpipe]."

R. R. wrote, "A young poet, whose verse is often

read [probably Victor Neuberg], astonished me by a graceful and beautiful dance, which he continued until he fell exhausted in the middle of the room, where he lay until the end."

Crowley then read an unpublished poem, which R. R. said was beautiful. This was followed by a dead silence. At this point the figure on the throne rose and played a violin "with passion and feeling—like a master."

Another silence followed the last strains of the music, after which an unseen voice declared the ceremonies ended.

The *Invocation to Luna* was so successful that Crowley expanded it into seven acts. One each was devoted to each of five planets, one to the sun, and another to the moon. Together they detailed the dramatic poetical search for occult wisdom. In the first invocation, the suppliant went to Saturn, the planet symbolizing old age. He asked for the riddle of man's existence. He was told that there is no God. He went in turn to Jupiter, Mars, the sun, Venus, and Mercury. He still did not learn what he wanted to know. Then in the seventh invocation, that of the moon, he found the virgin Moon enthroned like a madonna. Pagan Pan appeared and tore away a veil behind the goddess to reveal the Conquering Child of the Future.

It was Crowley's belief that two true magicians could beget a magical child with superhuman powers. He tried to do this with a number of women, but failed.

Newspaper reports of these invocations, which were held in London's Caxton Hall, were not as kind as the one R. R. wrote for the *Sketch.* One writer likened the costumes to those of attendants in a Turkish bath, and called the rituals gibberish. He noted with horror that Crowley flung back a curtain and declared that there is no God. "He then exhorts his followers to do as they like and make the most of this life." (This is the Law of Thelema.) The writer does admit that the violin playing was "not unskillful" and that Crowley's reading of Swinburne's poetry was effective.

"But," he added, "we leave it to our readers to say whether this is not a blasphemous sect whose proceedings conceivably lend themselves to immorality of the most revolting character. . . .

"New religion indeed! It is as old as the hills. It is the doctrine of unbridled lust and license based on the assumption that there is no God and no hereafter."

Another said that Crowley's poetry was remarkable, perfect in meter, rhythm, and melody, but often came near to the borderline of insanity. It was, the reviewer said, spoiled by "the intrusion of wild, erotic, and disgusting images and startling blasphemies, which restrict his writing to private circulation." The writer went on to say that now Crowley was preaching a "new religion," the propaganda for which consisted of "assembling a number of ladies and gentlemen in a dark room, where poems are recited in sonorous tones and a violin is played with considerable expression, amid clouds of choking incense, varied by barbaric dances, sensational interludes of melodrama, blasphemy, and erotic suggestion."

Crowley had no use for war and armies. So when World War I began in 1914, Crowley came to America. His reputation of being a devil worshiper and magician made him good copy for the newspapers as he traveled around the country.

Before the United States entered the war in April 1917, Crowley allied himself with pro-German forces in this country. In particular, he edited the *International,* a German propaganda paper. In one issue he is supposed to have written what was called an obscene attack upon King George of England. At the same time he conducted magical séances and was known as "The Purple Priest," after the gaudy gowns he wore.

He also became an associate of a secret society working to obtain Ireland's independence from Great Britain. This led him to make a dramatic exhibition at the foot of the Statue of Liberty on July 3, 1915. He went through the motions of throwing his British passport in the water (but did not really do so), and made a wild speech proclaiming an Irish republic. This was done before dawn and only some newspaper reporters and a few followers were there to hear him.

"In this dark moment," he cried, "before the father orb of our system [the sun] kindles with his kiss the sea, I swear the great oath of the revolution! . . . I renounce forever all allegiance to every alien tyrant. I swear to fight to the last drop of my blood to liberate the men and women of Ireland. I call upon the free people of this country, on whose hospitable shores I stand an exile, to give me countenance and assistance in my task of breaking the bonds which they broke for themselves one hundred and thirty-eight years ago.

"I proclaim the Irish Republic! I unfurl the Irish flag! Eire go Bragh! God save Ireland!"

This sounded very dramatic and indicated that poet Crowley would emulate poet Byron, who died fighting for Greek independence. However, Crowley was not a fighter in the physical sense. When the war ended, he went to Sicily in 1920, where he founded the Abbey of Thelema. Some very strange stories came out of Sicily about what went on in the Crowley order. According to one British paper, "The bestial orgies conducted by Aleister Crowley in Sicily sound like the ravings of a criminal lunatic, made mad by his own depravity. . . . The orgies are carried on as mystic religious rites in an old farmhouse near the village of Cefalu."

The story, supposedly built upon testimony given the newspaper by a woman who escaped from the Crowley order, said the magic rites were carried on in a large windowless room. A large orange circle was painted on the flat stone floor. There were interlaced black triangles inside the circle. The room was filled with incense made by burning goat's blood and honey. The rites were not described except in these general terms: "In this room are carried on unspeakable orgies, impossible of description. Suffice to say that they are horrible beyond the misgivings of decent people."

Crowley supporters have angrily denied the truth of this article. But after Raoul Loveday, a Crowley disciple, died under still unexplained circumstances, Sicilian authorities chose to believe the worst they heard about Crowley and his rites. Crowley's apologists still insist that Loveday probably died of food poisoning and not from the effects of a Crowley magick rite that went wrong, as Crowley's enemies have claimed.

However, even those who support Crowley admit that the magick practiced at the Abbey of Thelema was based upon tantric sex-magic. This derives from a less respectable form of Hinduism known as Lefthand Tantrism, which—in some sects—is involved with worship of Kali, the bloody consort of Siva in his role of the Destroyer of Life.

Crowley was expelled from Sicily and returned to England in 1923, after a short time in France and Tunisia. He suffered greatly in trying to break himself of addiction to heroin. He is said to have succeeded in breaking the habit, but the painful struggle left him exhausted and broke. The fortune left him by his father was gone.

He moved into a house at Hastings in Sussex. It is a tribute to British ability to forgive that he was permitted to return at all. Here he continued to write books and dream of reestablishing a new Abbey of Thelema. To the end of his life he gloried in being known as "The Beast 666," which his mother conferred on him, and the "wickedest man in the world," which newspapers called him after revelations of the Sicily rites were published. He died at Hastings in 1947 at the age of seventy-two. He was cremated and his ashes divided among his disciples, many in the United States, especially Southern California.

Aleister Crowley was a dope addict, a sex maniac, and a moral anarchist. He was also a sincere magician in the grand tradition. He drew his pentagrams and hexagrams and recited the ancient formulae. He saw visions as a result. How much of these were self-delusion and how much were voices from beyond is something that cannot be determined.

Of all the great magicians of whom we have anything like accurate and believable records, Aleister Crowley seems to be the only one besides Edward Kelley who wanted to be evil for evil's sake. Even Faust, of both legend and literature, was seeking knowledge rather than evil when he sought the Devil's aid. In fact, most really great magicians have been religious at heart. Many who retreated from religion in the course of their magical pursuits returned to religion in the end.

Crowley was not one of these. He carried his wickedness to the end. While everything about Crowley is controversial, it may have been this love of evil that defeated him as a magician. There is no reason to believe that the occult is evil, as we generally understand the meaning of the word. In fact, cabalistic magic is based upon esoteric biblical secrets. As such, it would hardly be evil if honestly based upon truth.

There is no denying Crowley's brilliance in his early life. He began as a true student of magic and was convinced that he was the reincarnation of Eliphas Lévi, who was himself a sincere student. But later Crowley's view began to change. He became more interested in the wildest kind of earthly pleasure and in things that ordinary people call evil. His studies in the blacker side of magic naturally brought him to Edward Kelley, John Dee's evil genius. Crowley was fascinated by Kelley's story. His studies of Kelley led Crowley to the belief that he was also a reincarnation of Kelley. The Elizabethan sage's amoral philosophy exactly fitted Crowley's own attitude toward life and the world in general.

In seeking evil for evil's sake, Crowley may have blinded himself to real truth that his communion with astral beings might have imparted to him. However, it must be admitted that much of Crowley's reputation for being an evil man depends upon the interpretations of his own time. Today many of the things he did would not be considered so bad. Also, he delighted in making himself appear worse than he really was.

But the crucial question is: Was he a real magician? It does not seem so. Yet, at least in his younger years, he tried earnestly. Even if we concede that he was a faker in the end, we must give him credit for trying.

❖12❖

The Devil Worshipers

Devil worshipers, satanists, diabolists, and whatever else one may choose to call them, are not magicians, although magicians may—as Faust did—turn to satanism when straight magic fails.

True magic goes beyond worshiping the Devil for what material gain one can get out of it. Just as Lévi and others tried to tell us that organized religion is but a simple, childish way to explain the true state of the infinite, satanism must be considered in the same light. For actually, satanism merely substitutes Satan for God as someone to worship.

Satanism is often referred to as black magic. White magic is considered to be magical rituals devoted to expanding the concept of God beyond the confines of religion. Fundamental religionists see no difference between the two and call them both black magic.

Be that as it may, those who worship Satan often use

magic rituals in their services. Here again, when one gets into satanism there are two clearly marked divisions. There are those who conduct satanic rites because they are genuinely evil people. There are plenty of examples of this—the evil fifteenth-century Gilles de Rais who murdered a ghastly number of children to use their blood in his infernal magic; the ritual murder of Sharon Tate, the Hollywood star, by the half-crazed Manson family; and exposure of sickening rites among teenagers and adults in Waukegan, Illinois, in 1972, among many other cases.

On the other hand, there are those who study satanism as an extension of knowledge, with no evil designs attached to it at all. Faust was not an evil man, outside of the fact that he rejected God for the Devil's aid. He wanted knowledge. When he could not get it any other way, he succumbed to Mephistopheles' temptations. John Dee was another Faust in this respect. He hungered for knowledge, turning to the angels when he could not find what he wanted in books. When angel magic failed him, he was dragged into the more sinister pursuits of the Mephistophelean Edward Kelley.

Often those who seek a liaison with Satan through diabolism turn back to orthodox religion in the end. One such was Joris-Karl Huysman (1848–1907), a famous writer of the French decadent school. Huysman wrote one of the most graphic descriptions of the satanic Black Mass ever put on paper.

Huysman had been experimenting in magic and became acquainted with satanism. He became very interested in this darker side of magic and decided to base his next book upon it. When he asked around among his friends for someone who could give him authentic instruction, he was told to appeal to the Abbé Boullan.

Boullan, an unfrocked priest, had seemed headed for a distinguished career in the Church. However, in concert with a young nun, he began to dabble in magic. This ended with accusations that brought him a short prison term. He received absolution after his sentence and continued in the Church until 1875, when another clash with his superiors caused him to leave the Church. Boullan then joined the magician Vintras. Later he became head of Vintras' order when the older magician died. Rejected by most of Vintras' followers, he formed his own order. Before long it was being whispered about that the former priest was now one of the blackest of black magicians.

This was exactly the kind of man Huysman sought. He said that he wanted no crooks or frauds. He wanted a genuine magician, admitting that satanic magic "possesses a mystery that appeals to me."

He wrote to Boullan, who answered cautiously. But after Huysman explained what he wanted, Boullan agreed to supply the novelist with authentic material about satanism, which he claimed was stronger than it had been since the Middle Ages.

This resulted in Huysman's famous novel *Là-Bas,* which appeared first as a serial in *Echo de Paris,* a newspaper. It is partly autobiographical, for the protagonist is—like Huysman—a young novelist named

Durtal who wishes to write a book about satanism and particularly about the notorious Gilles de Rais. Huysman brings his hero together with a mysterious occultist named des Hermies, who supplies the young man with occult books and materials in the same manner that Boullan supported Huysman.

Among the books Durtal, the novelist, receives from his magician friend are the works of Eliphas Lévi. Durtal—as Huysman also did—found them frustrating because Lévi failed to follow through to the final important facts. Throughout the book Huysman wove in actual people, under different names, so that the effect is extraordinarily real. The book has a distinct "this really happened" effect upon the reader, which accounts for its great popularity.

From an occult standpoint, the most important part of the book is an extremely realistic account of a satanic Black Mass that the hero attends in company with a woman devotee who gains entrance for him. After Huysman's death, some of his friends claimed that he actually witnessed such a satanic ceremony as conducted by Boullan. Other friends denied this and claimed the account was either fictional or based upon information given him by Boullan.

Regardless, Huysman gave a terrifyingly realistic picture of a satanic mass, made all the more real because real people were identifiable beneath their fictional names. His description of Docre, the satanic priest, is Boullan in every way. Hyacinthe, the woman who takes Durtal to the Black Mass, described Docre as a priest about whom terrible things were said. He had been confessor to a queen and then had been driven from the Church for his unholy activities and excommunicated. Several times he had been accused of poisoning people in his blasphemous rites, but had never been convicted. He was accompanied by a middle-aged woman who supposedly had second sight. Hyacinthe ended by saying the man was depraved—but utterly charming.

In the story, an old man who was painted and powdered let them into the temple. He took them into a room fitted up as a chapel. It was extremely hot there and smelled of decay and dampness. The place was dimly lit by gas lights behind rose-colored glass. There were some spectators in the room, but all seemed nervous or extremely serious. Durtal observed to his companion that Satan did not seem to make his followers happy.

The disgusting-looking old man, dressed as an altar boy, came and lighted candles in the back of the room. This revealed an altar like that of any church, except the image of Christ behind it was sickeningly obscene. The candles were black and smelled of tar as they burned.

Next a skeleton-thin altar boy, dressed in red, lighted candles in tripods at each side of the altar, throwing in leaves and perfumes in a ceremony as old as magic itself. Hyacinthe explained that the material being burned was plants whose scents were agreeable to Satan—"Our Master."

At this point Docre entered, dressed in a long red gown. He wore a priest's biretta with two buffalo horns attached to it, simulating the horns of Satan. Docre was tall, with heavy, lined features. His eyes were small and dark, and appeared phosphorescent—they reminded Durtal of a cat's.

The black priest bowed, and Durtal saw that under his vestments Docre was naked. He went to the altar. The ceremony began as an almost exact imitation of the Catholic Low Mass, but was interrupted by acolytes who took smoking bowls around for the worshipers to smell—probably it was hashish. The priest then knelt and cried:

"Master of scandals! Giver of crime's rewards! Prince of sins and magnificent vices! Satan, it is thou whom we adore!"

He went on to beseech Satan's aid in giving his worshipers the gifts of hypocrisy, cunning, and pride so they could defend themselves against the children of God.

"Lord of the despised, Satan! . . . . Your worshipers beseech you on our knees. Help us obtain the exquisite joys of crimes undiscovered by the law. Help us do evil deeds. From you, King of the Dispossessed—the son whom the inflexible Father drove out of heaven—we cry for Glory, Wealth, and Power!"

Docre then rose to his feet. His begging tones turned to fury and hate as he began to revile Jesus Christ as a stealer of worship He had no right to. He cursed Him as one who had forgotten the poverty-stricken, and damned the popes who served religion. As his curses grew wilder, the altar boys interrupted with a chorus of amens. The filth and blasphemy reached a crescendo. Then the altar boys rang bells. The worshipers became as if possessed, leaping, rolling on the floor, some making weird sounds and some voiceless. Docre paid no attention to the actions of the worshipers, who acted like the medieval conception of a witches' sabbat on Walpurgis Night. He turned and spat on the crucifix. The wild melee then turned into a sexual orgy of the most depraved kind.

Durtal was so sickened that he almost fainted. He rushed from the room, unable to bear the sacrilege any longer.

The book was published in 1891, following its newspaper serialization, and was highly successful. Ever since its publication, there has been a literary argument about Huysman's own participation in satanism. There has been no argument, however, about the accuracy of Huysman's picture of the Black Mass.

The evidence points to his not only having attended such magical ceremonies, but having been a satanist himself, at least for a while. We do know that he did not break off his association with Boullan as he should have done if his only interest was in writing *Là Bas*. He continued corresponding with the magician until Boullan died in 1893.

There was too deep a religious streak in Huysman for him to embrace satanism for long, although he was fascinated by it and by Boullan. However, he believed in magic and in the reality of malicious spirits. He was convinced that evil spirits were attacking him because of his book. He got Boullan to prepare for him paste wafers that he could burn to exorcise these spirits when they bothered him.

It seems strange that Boullan, as a worshiper of the Devil, would furnish means of exorcism, which normally would be the work of special priests of the Catholic Church. However, in this case, he seems to have turned against his satanic master. Huysman said the tablets were compounded of myrrh, an odd form of incense, camphor, and cloves. When Huysman felt the spirits about him, he burned one of the tablets by placing it on red-hot coals from the fireplace in his room. This caused smoke and a strong mixture of perfume and camphor in the air. The evil spirits found this stifling and were driven away. Huysman also had to stand inside a magic circle and recite a special ritual that Boullan gave him.

After Boullan's death in 1893, Huysman became increasingly fearful of satanic forces. He turned back to the Catholic Church and ended his days as an oblate (dedicated to monastic life without actually becoming a monk) attached to a Benedictine monastery.

The type of satanism revealed by Huysman and practiced by Boullan is thoroughly evil and is magic practiced for no other reason than doing evil. The practitioner is on the same level as the witch doctor and the voodoo devotee. However, there is another side of satanism that claims to avoid the evil aspects of the darker devil sects. Anton Szandor LaVey, pastor of the Church of Satan and author of *The Satanic Bible,* is one of these.

LaVey, who was called Harold Levy back in Chicago where he was born in 1930, studied music, but preferred a more adventurous life. He joined the Clyde Beatty circus, assisting Beatty in the lion act. Later he left the circus and traveled for several years with carnivals. This was followed by three years as a police photographer for the San Francisco Police Department. He left this to work as a professional organist. Then in 1966—the year he now designates as 1 Anno Satanas—he formed his Church of Satan with himself as high priest.

Satanism was certainly not new when LaVey announced his church, but this was the first time anyone had openly established such a temple. In the first years of the Church of Satan, LaVey depended upon his background in the circus, the carnival, and as a stage magician to put on a good show. This and his open declarations brought him a flood of publicity, written by reporters intrigued both by the name of the church and by such showmanship as LaVey's using a nude woman's body as an altar.

By 1972 LaVey claimed seventeen thousand members for his satanic church and had grown more conservative. Becoming very selective, he no longer welcomed anyone for membership. He claimed that in the opening years, the bizarre publicity attracted many freaks and hippie types who were seeking only fun and novelty. Today the membership supposedly is predominantly serious and middle-class. There are professors, law enforcement people, middle-level businessmen, and a large number of military people. More radical occultists consider LaVey too tame.

In the introduction to LaVey's *The Satanic Bible,* Michael A. Aquino denies that witchcraft and old-time magic are merely "a neurotic reaction against the established religious disciplines." He says that satanism is not "devil worship." It rejects the worship of all deities. The basic tenet seems to be that one should do as he or she wishes—a sort of modern restating of Aleister Crowley's Law of Thelema. Yet LaVey's regard for law and order seems to argue against this belief. Actually, what he seems to be saying is that as long as one does not infringe upon the freedom of others, then one should follow his or her own inclinations, for there is no sin.

The Church of Satan is not the only such organization. The so-called occult explosion that began in the 1960s brought a bewildering proliferation of groups, orders, and "churches." Many of these are out-and-out frauds. Many may be partially sincere, although differing from each other. We might liken today's magicians to the blind men who tried to describe an elephant. One touched the beast's trunk and declared it was like a snake. Another touched its leg and said it was built of pillars—and so on. Magic is such an infinite subject that no teacher or writer has ever done more than feel its trunk or its leg or its belly and formed his opinion of the whole from this individual part. Magicians through the centuries have done the same thing that Lévi complained of about theologians. They have given us parables and fables—showing us the clothing and skin of magic rather than the blood and the bones hidden inside.

The great magicians of the past—the true occult scholars—have all hinted or said that they had more knowledge than they put in their books, for the truth is too dangerous to be passed along to any except those sufficiently versed in magic to protect themselves. However, a study of their lives and their failures to achieve superhuman status, which magic is supposed to confer, indicates strongly that they did not know the ultimate secrets. They may have known more than the average person—even quite a bit more of the unknown—but they were still blind men describing an elephant by feel.

If any had the true secrets of magic, then Paracelsus could have banished all diseases and Lévi would not have had to associate with radical socialists. He could have waved his wand and brought about the social changes he advocated. Faust would have done more than perform some conjuror's tricks. Roger Bacon would have built submarines, flying machines, and other wonders in the thirteenth century instead of just predicting them. And Aleister Crowley might have been emperor of the world instead of a drug-sodden leader of a small group.

Occult means concealed and, in another sense, that

which is beyond human understanding. This means that there definitely is an occult. All the secrets of life, death, and the interrelation of man and the universe are still concealed—and possibly in our present mental stage of development, beyond understanding. In this sense, the occult is simply the normal state of creation whose concept is still beyond our human ability to comprehend. We cannot see it, just as we cannot see light and radiations except in a narrow band to which our eyesight is attuned. What unearthly colors might exist if one could see radiations beyond the visible spectrum? And what unearthly things may exist beyond our sight, feel, and hearing? All that Mejnour, the magician of Bulwer-Lytton's *Zanoni*, did was to show the invisible world to his student.

In a strictly scientific application of magic, the magician is trying to contact minds on other planes of creation in the same manner that scientists of the conventional type are using radio telescopes to listen in on sounds of the universe created by the stars.

There is no reason why it cannot be done mentally. The seeker only has to have the power to receive, *if* those he seeks have superhuman mental powers. The entire idea of crystal gazing is not to see real images in the glass, but to focus the mind—as a bright moving object is sometimes used to focus a subject's attention in hypnotism—and shut out earthly distractions. Then all attention is focused upon the matter in hand—that is, opening the mind to receive cosmic vibrations.

This is what the true magician—the occult scientist—

is doing with his rituals. He is focusing his mind upon the infinite. But does he really see or feel something from the other side? It is possible that he does—but he cannot explain it to the rest of us.

This is because we are in the same mental prison as the caveman trying to explain a rock that fell without visible reason. We can only comprehend and describe by comparison. If what the magician sees and feels happens to be something entirely new to human vision, experience, and philosophy, he will not be able to describe it to us, even if he understands it himself. This does not mean that the unknown will always remain unknown. The human mind is expanding from generation to generation, moving closer to the time when it will finally be able to comprehend the stupendous nature of time and space.

Thus, the magician is justified in using his mind to explore the unknown. However, those who depend upon drugs, bestial rites, sex-magic, and any other means that gratify human hungers are not true occult scientists. They are self-centered egotists seeking only to find magical secrets to satisfy their own cravings. The things they seek are already known. But the true occult scientist is concerned with the unknown. As the scryer at his crystal ball must put aside the distracting images of the world and open his mind to receive the vibrations from occult space, so must the magician's rituals serve only to focus his or her mind upon the great Beyond in hope that there is something there to send communications—and that the human mind has the capability to receive them if they should be sent.

Used in this sense, magic has a definite place in true scientific investigation of the mysteries of creation. In the last few years, parapsychology has become a respectable science. The human mind still remains the greatest of all tools. Giant computers, able to solve astronomically complex equations, still cannot work without human programming.

The magician is working with his own mind. If he is a true occult scientist, and not a hedonistic fraud like Crowley, then he deserves our respect—whether we believe in his results or not.

Bibliography

Bulwer-Lytton, Edward, *Zanoni*. Boston, Little, Brown & Co., 1897.

Christian, Paul, *The History and Practice of Magic*. New York, Citadel Press, reprinted 1969.

Dumas, Francoise R., *Cagliostro*. New York, Orion Press, 1967.

Edmonds, I.G., *The Magic Makers*. New York, Thomas Nelson Inc., 1976.

Edmonds, I. G., *Second Sight*. New York, Thomas Nelson Inc., 1977.

French, Peter T., *John Dee*. London, Routledge & Kegan Paul, 1972.

Houdini (Erich Weiss), *Unmasking Robert Houdin*. New York, Publishers Printing Company, 1908.

LaVey, Anton S., *The Satanic Bible*. Secaucus, N.J., University Books, 1968.

Lévi, Eliphas, (A.E. Waite, tr.) *The History of Magic*. New York, Samuel Weiser, reprinted 1973 (original edition 1913).

McIntosh, Christopher, *Eliphas Lévi and the French Occult Revival*. New York, Samuel Weiser, 1972.

Rohmer, Sax, (Arthur Ward), *The Romance of Sorcery*. New York, E. P. Dutton, 1914.

192 | *The Kings of Black Magic*

Rose, William, ed., *The History of the Damnable Life and Deserved Death of Dr. John Faust.* London, George Routledge and Sons.

Sheed, F. J., ed., *Soundings in Satanism.* New York, Sheed and Ward, 1972.

Van Ash, Cay, and Rohmer, Elizabeth, *Master of Villainy.* Bowling Green, Ohio, Bowling Green University Popular Press, 1972.

Index

About the Author

I.G. EDMONDS was born in Texas, but now makes his home in California. He was a newspaper reporter and then spent twenty-one years in the U.S. Air Force. Since retiring from the service, he has written over ninety books, about half of which have been for young people. He has traveled widely, investigating occult subjects in many lands. This research has gone into such books as *D.D. Home, Second Sight, Other Lives* and *The Girls Who Talked to Ghosts.*